MW00612150

LIFT HIGH THE CROSS

✝

LIFT HIGH
THE
CROSS

A History of the
TRINITY EPISCOPAL
SCHOOL FOR MINISTRY

Training New Leaders to
Make Christ Known

Janet Leighton

Harold Shaw Publishers
Wheaton, Illinois

Copyright ©1995 by Janet Leighton

All rights reserved. No part of this book may be reproduced or transmitted in any form or by any means, electronic or mechanical, including photocopying, recording, or any information storage and retrieval system without written permission from Harold Shaw Publishers, Box 567, Wheaton, Illinois 60189. Printed in the United States of America. All Scripture quotations, unless otherwise indicated, are taken from The Holy Bible: New International Version. Copyright ©1973, 1978, 1984 by the International Bible Society. Used by permission of Zondervan Publishing House. All rights reserved.

ISBN 0-87788-474-9

Cover design by David LaPlaca

Library of Congress Cataloging-in-Publication Data

Leighton, Janet, 1956-

Lift high the cross : the story of Trinity Episcopal School for Ministry / Janet Leighton

   p.   cm.

Includes index.

ISBN 0-87788-474-9

1. Trinity Episcopal School for Ministry (Ambridge, Pa.)--History. 2. Ambridge (Pa.)--Church history--20th century.

BV4070.T718L45 1995

207'.1'13--dc20   95-46375

99 98 97 96 95

10 9 8 7 6 5 4 3 2 1

Acknowledgements

I am grateful to the many people who contributed to this book:

John Rodgers gave unqualified support and encouragement from the time I presented the idea to him.

John Guest helped me to recognize God's call to write the book.

Bill Frey and the Board, the faculty, and the staff of Trinity Episcopal School for Ministry (TESM) gave me open access to minutes, Self-Study reports, issues of <u>Seed and Harvest</u>, personal interviews, and tapes.

Marjory Stanway and Nanky Chalfant shared their love and their dedication to the Lord Jesus Christ and to TESM, as well as their own experience in writing books.

Gerry and Althea Dorman, and Paul and Susie Leighton read the manuscript and offered helpful suggestions.

Eleanor Miller and her staff completed the typesetting.

Steve Board, of Harold Shaw Publishers, guided me step by step through the mechanics of publication.

My husband and best friend, Christopher, helped me to keep my hand to the plow.

I offer my sincere thanks to each one.

Foreword

It is both a privilege and a personal joy for me to write an introduction to this book which tells much of the story of the founding and the development of the Trinity Episcopal School for Ministry. It does not, of course, pretend to offer an exhaustive acount nor to tell of all who played a significant part in the schools history.

Having lived through the days and events of this account, I can assure the reader that Janet Leighton, herself a graduate and the wife of a graduate of Trinity, has caught the spirit and adventure of the school. With deft strokes, at a fast-moving pace, she touches upon key figures and chief events used by God to do a marvelous work in beginning and developing this school.

Above all, as I read this account, I was struck anew by the overruling grace of God, the Christian maturity and sanctity of Bishop Alfred Stanway, and the spiritual challenge and wisdom, or practical helpfulness, which we all received from him and from Mrs. Stanway. The reader will find much of this practical piety and challenge awaiting him or her in this book. This will prove to be a book to be read numerous times with personal profit. To approximate Charles Simeon: "It will glorify God, humble the sinner, and encourage the saint."

In commending this book to you most highly, I wish to thank Janet Leighton for her considerable work, for her perseverance, and for her faithfulness to a divine call in providing us this book, researched and written in the midst of a very busy family and parish life.

The Very Rev. Dr. John H. Rodgers, Jr.

Dean and President Emeritus, Trinity Episcopal School for Ministry, Director Emeritus, Stanway Institute for World Mission and Evangelism, Professor for Systematic Theology, Trinity Episcopal School for Ministry
28 Pentecost ,
Ambridge, PA

Table of Contents

1
A Standing Ovation

The tall, young preacher from Sewickley, Pennsylvania rose to answer a question. His gaze swept across the expectant crowd of two thousand that packed the cathedral in Atlanta. Choosing his words carefully, measuring their full effect, the Rev. John Guest announced, "We in the Fellowship of Witness are committed to seeing the establishment of a new seminary in the Episcopal Church, one that will be thoroughly biblical and evangelical."

He went on to say that a temporary board had been formed, and was about to invite a prominent leader to be the first Dean and President.

The throng, gathered for a National Episcopal Conference on Renewal in October of 1974, sprang to a standing ovation. The applause resounded on and on.

The Rt. Rev. John Howe, then Associate Rector at St. Stephen's, Sewickley, remembers that the other business of the conference seemed to pale in significance. The prospect of a new school inspired the remainder of the week.

"I was just a young rector," reflected John Guest, some fifteen years later. "I was relatively unknown. I wasn't doing any national speaking of any consequence. So, to have them all stand and applaud was a stunning result for me.

"It was the first significant gathering of all the renewal ministries in the Episcopal Church, and so we were delighted to be together and discover each other. Somebody must have known where the network was, in order to gather all those people. But most of us had no real awareness."

In fact, God had quietly been igniting fires of conversion and renewal in individuals for years. Now He was bringing His people together, and introducing them to each other.

The Beginnings of Renewal

With the growing upheaval in American society in the twentieth century, many in the Church stressed the need to address the ills of the culture. In the process, however, there was a gradual shift away from the priority of calling people to conversion and faith in the Lord Jesus Christ. Consequently, many seminaries and clergy abandoned the authority of Holy Scripture as the supreme guide for life and doctrine. They were placing less and less emphasis on the "evangel", the core of the Gospel, the Good News that salvation was made possible through the death of Jesus Christ.

In the 1960's, some new movements began to spring up. In California, the Rev. Dennis Bennett received "the baptism in the Holy Spirit" with speaking in tongues. He searched the Bible for an understanding of his "charismatic" experience and began to speak and teach about the power of the Holy Spirit in the lives of those who loved Jesus.

One who came to learn from him was the Rev. Terry Fullam. Through prayer, he also experienced the release of the Spirit, and called others to know the God of the Bible as the One who is still at work in the twentieth century. His parish, St. Paul's Church in Darien, Connecticut, grew rapidly as people hungry for his message flocked to the congregation.

Through these and other leaders, individuals scattered around the country also began to experience personal "renewal". With a new thirst to walk in a close relationship with God, they began to gather in groups to study the Bible and to pray. And they were motivated to witness, to share with other people the significant transformation occurring in their lives.

Movements such as Faith Alive and Cursillo began to attract seekers. Led mostly by lay people who had come to a new loyalty to the risen Lord Jesus, these groups were the vehicle for bringing still others to a personal relationship with Him.

Of the many lay people disenchanted with liberalism and experiencing renewal, a growing number were sensing a call to the ordained ministry. And even those who did not discern such a call were eager to grow in a Scripturally-based theological understanding of their faith.

Meanwhile, in 1963, a small American branch of the Evangelical Fellowship in the Anglican Church (EFAC) had been formed. "Evangelical" Episcopalians had experienced their "golden age" in the eighteen thirties and forties, when the influence from the Great Awakening remained strong. Their number had dwindled until they were a scattered minority, clinging to the Bible as the only authority for faith and doctrine. They believed in the sinless life of Jesus Christ and His substitutionary atonement, His death on the cross in the place of sinners so that they might be reconciled to the Father. They affirmed His bodily resurrection, glorious ascension, triumphant reign, and future return. They held that sinful human beings were justified, made right with God, only through faith in Jesus Christ. They felt it was incumbent upon them to share this message of salvation with all who did not believe.

Founded by Dr. Philip E. Hughes and the Rev. Peter Moore and called the Fellowship of Witness (FOW), this group's main purpose was to foster education, hand-in-hand with evangelism. It was felt that education alone was not enough to make committed disciples; it might lead to "correct" thinking, but it could not guarantee a vibrant faith. On the other hand, evangelism alone would foster enthusiastic experiences devoid of the Scriptural undergirding necessary for preventing spiritual chaos. But the combination of education and evangelism would equip Christians to fulfill the Great Commission of Jesus, "Go and make disciples of all nations" (Matthew 28:20).

To that end, the FOW began to gather a mailing list of sympathizers, mostly lay people, and sought ways to influence the Episcopal Church for the gospel of Jesus Christ. It organized national and regional conferences. It began to publish educational materials. Its members conscientiously worked to raise up new leaders.

Gradually, a handful of key individuals began to identify with the movement. By the early 1970's, John Guest and John Howe had emerged as leaders. As their parish, St. Stephen's in Sewickley, became more and more influential, the FOW was able to reach a larger following.

At the same time, however, some found the atmosphere in the Episcopal Church too hostile to renewal. "We lost a lot of good people in the late sixties and early seventies", remembered John Guest, "people who **were** Episcopalians, who took off and went somewhere else. I remember walking along with one man, pleading with him not to leave the Episcopal Church. He did it anyway. When that keeps happening, the larger environment has to change."

FOW soon realized that it would not be able to change the Church without changing clergy. And so theological education emerged as a priority.

John Guest and John Howe pursued the idea of creating an Anglo-American Training Program. The plan was to build an arrangement whereby American students would go to England to study theology from an evangelical perspective, and English students would come to the United States to train in a practicum. At first, it seemed like a workable idea, but it became clear that the English were not that interested in a cross-cultural experience.

Similarly, Peter Moore had been steering individual students toward England. As they approached him for advice concerning evangelical training, he suggested that they go to England for a solid foundation in Biblical theology, and return to America for the obligatory year at an Episcopal seminary. But as an increasing number of interested people approached him, it was evident that the situation warranted a school here.

As Famous For God As For Steel

At the same time that the Spirit of God was moving this handful of people to dream and pray about a new Episcopal seminary, He had been creating a favorable spiritual climate in Pittsburgh.

In the early 1950's, Baptist minister Kathryn Kuhlman began holding meetings in the auditorium of the city's Carnegie Library. Through her preaching and the gift of healing that He had given her, the Holy Spirit brought literally thousands of people to conversion over more than two decades. Several books were written containing the stories, documented and verified medically, of individuals whom God had dramatically healed. People were seeing right in their own city that God's power was just as visibly active in the twentieth century as it had been in the first.

Meanwhile in the Episcopal Church, Austin Pardue, Bishop of Pittsburgh from 1944 to 1968, was a figure known nationally for his books on prayer. And Emily Gardiner Neal, who had been hired by *Redbook* magazine to unmask fraud in the healing movement, became convinced that it was a genuine work of God. She, in turn, helped many others to know the Lord as she wrote up her research in the book, *A Reporter Finds God*. She subsequently authored many other books on healing.

And in 1952, the Rev. Dr. Samuel Moor Shoemaker left a dynamic ministry in New York City to become the rector of Calvary Episcopal Church in the East Liberty section of Pittsburgh. He soon articulated a vision for making the city "as famous for God as it is for steel".

He began to meet with a group made up mostly of lay people from different denominations. They came together regularly to read Scripture and pray, and to talk about the needs of the city. Often, Dr. Shoemaker would lead discussion on a specific issue.

This group came to be known as the Pittsburgh Offensive. Though never officially incorporated, it did gradually develop a number of specialized ministries in the Pittsburgh area.

One of Dr. Shoemaker's strategies was to reach out to the polished "Golf Club crowd". These successful, self-reliant young men were emerging leaders in the business world. Many were members of his new congregation, but they felt disenfranchised from the church. The Christianity that they knew seemed to have no meaningful connection with daily life.

In this spiritual vacuum, Dr. Shoemaker began to meet with them in small groups. As he shared about a living faith in a living God, he challenged them to start praying about the circumstances of their lives. As individuals undertook thirty-day "experiments" of prayer, they found, to their amazement, that God heard and answered. They noticed changes beginning to take place, both in themselves, and in the people and situations for which they had prayed. This small-group movement soon developed into a vital force known as the Pittsburgh Experiment, which continues to this day, focusing on the need to apply the Christian faith in ministry to the marketplace.

In addition, there were outreach ministries to college students and to the unemployed. Weekly radio programs were carried on a major station. Later, a foundation was developed to serve as a conduit for funds and as a point of accountability.

In 1974, R.C. Sproul was part of that community of Christian leadership, the Pittsburgh Offensive. He began to challenge John Guest and John Howe. Perhaps God was leading them to go beyond just an Anglo-American Training Program. Maybe He had a much bigger plan, one that would include more people, and would have a wider effect on the Church. What would they do if He were calling them to start a full-blown school for training leaders?

For John Guest, the moment of decision stands out vividly.

"I remember being in the shower, in tremendous anguish, dreaming for God to do something significant to change the Church at large. In great turmoil of soul, I prayed and brought the whole matter before the Lord, and then made the commitment, 'I'm going to go for it. I'm going to lay my life, my energy, on the line for this new project.'"

God Pays For What He Orders

Clearly God had given this small group a vision, but so far there was not a cent to pay for it. John began to call around to scattered Episcopalians that he knew of across the country. He was trying to get some idea of the financial support that might be available for this new venture. Many were interested, but one person in particular, Nancy Chalfant, was deeply moved.

Years later, she commented, "The whole vision of a school for ministry in which future leaders would be trained to teach the Word of God was exactly what I, as a lay person, felt was needed in the Church. I had had a spiritual experience years before in which I had come to know God, to love Jesus Christ, and to know He loved me, but my understanding was not nurtured with faithful teaching from the Scriptures. I did a lot of reading and exploring of spiritual things—some good, some dangerous—but I didn't realize that my whole Christian walk was out of balance.

"Only later, after I had come under John Guest's faithful preaching and teaching of the Word of God, did I become grounded in the Scriptures. As I looked back and saw all the wrong directions I had been going in, the Lord showed me how dangerous it could be not to have the theological underpinnings from the Word. I even felt cheated by the Church, because I had not received the proper nourishment.

"In my observation, seminaries seemed to be going in the wrong direction, too. They were not teaching clergy to help people like me to understand their spiritual experiences, or the importance of living by the Word of God.

"So when John Guest and John Howe approached me, I was very intrigued with the idea. The funny thing was that I had recently been in a discussion following a class in which it was brought up that people with more wealth don't often give sacrificially. We may give large amounts of money, but it doesn't usually cost us too much. And I realized that I had never really given sacrificially.

"I remember standing in John Guest's office with him and John Howe. We stood in a circle, holding hands, and praying. And I knew in my heart that giving the money to start the new school was something I would like to do."

God had given His people a vision. It had seemed right, but it would be very costly. Believing that God pays for what He orders, they had prayed that He would raise up the necessary funds. And He moved Nancy to meet the need. Her substantial gift was enough to launch the project.

Doing The Next Thing Next

John Guest went to a leading layman in his parish, Nancy's husband, Henry Chalfant, who was the Treasurer of the Diocese of Pittsburgh. He asked him, "If you were going to start a school for ministry, what would be your first steps?'

Henry answered, "I would go and see my Bishop, and I would go and see the Presiding Bishop."

"John Guest called me up one day," remembered Robert Appleyard, Bishop of Pittsburgh from 1968-1981. "He said he wanted to come talk about a school for ministry. He would be bringing a friend with him. I asked who that would be, and he responded, 'John Stott'.

"So they came into my office, and John Stott presented me with his latest book. I hadn't read it, but I did recognize him as a real leader in the Church, and I met him with joy."

The Bishop questioned John Guest closely, "Why a 'school for ministry', and not a 'seminary'?"

John was forthright in his conviction, "Seminary is not a good place to train ministers. Seminarians need, in order to go out and exercise ministry, some experience in the ministry that enlarges their own vision. It's downright hopeless to train ministers in seminary because the model is academic, not ministry-oriented. They talk 'ministry', but basically, it's a grind to get through three years and come out with a divinity degree."

The Bishop then began to raise all the questions that he felt a bishop ought to raise. Having been on the Board of Theological Education of the Episcopal Church (later, its chairman), and chairman of the Board of the General Theological Seminary in New York, he was well-acquainted with the troubles currently facing Episcopal seminaries.

"What about costs?" he asked. "You may have some start-up funds, but the amount of money that is needed grows rapidly as a school grows. What about personnel? Where will you find the necessary qualified faculty? What about students? It will take daring students to risk such an adventure! Who will ordain them?" He suggested that they go do their homework concerning establishing a chair of evangelism at an existing seminary. Perhaps it would be a better use of resources not to duplicate other efforts.

Later, the Bishop mused, "I sensed that John felt it would take ten to twenty-five years to go that route. He seemed to be saying, 'The time is right! The time is now!' So I suggested that they go see the Presiding Bishop."

"A group of us did go," said John Guest, "to see Bishop John Allin, who had just become the Presiding Bishop. We spent two hours with him one day in September of 1974. Bishop Allin also thought that a better use of that money would be to endow a chair for evangelism at Virginia [Theological] Seminary. We said that that money could just get absorbed in an endowment and that somebody could be appointed to an evangelism position who wasn't actually committed to evangelism.

"And he made this statement which was very encouraging. 'If you have the sense that God is calling you to do this, then even though it doesn't seem wise to me, I know that you have to go and pursue that call.'"

Peter Moore, who had accompanied John to New York, also went to see the Rev. John Coburn, who had been dean of the seminary he attended. The Rev. Coburn was then the president of the House of Clerical and Lay Deputies, one of the governing bodies of the national Church.

"When I told him what we had told Bishop Allin," recalls Peter, "he surprised me by saying, 'If you look historically, you'll see that every renewal movement has established its own seminary, and there's no reason why this one shouldn't.' I took his comments as another sign of encouragement from God."

One Door Closes, Another Opens

Shortly after it had become clear that an Anglo-American Training Program wouldn't work out, the group from FOW tried to buy the Philadelphia Divinity School (PDS), one of the old Episcopal seminaries, located in downtown Philadelphia. That school was preparing to close, but the buildings were in good shape.

John Guest called the Board of PDS while it was meeting in Philadelphia, and asked about buying those facilities. Several times he telephoned the agency that had been commissioned to sell the property, but he never got a call back.

By the fall, it seemed wise to locate in the Pittsburgh area because there were so many opportunities available for seminarians to have practical training for ministry. God also appeared to be guiding towards renting a temporary facility, which could accommodate the school in its beginning stages. Then, the available money could be invested in staff, student scholarships, and program, rather than in property.

With a clearer idea of where God was leading, but with many questions still unanswered, John Guest and Peter Moore went off to the renewal conference in Atlanta.

The Holy Spirit had mobilized this small group of praying individuals. He had given them a dream, and had helped them to find like-minded people in each other. He had used a variety of circumstances to confirm to them that He really was guiding them. Now it was time for them to make their intentions public.

"We were hoping to make an announcement at the conference about our plans for a school for ministry," said Peter Moore, "but we were very unsure what the response would be. We wanted to find the right time.

"And then John broke the news in answer to a question from the floor during a plenary session. The groundswell of support just amazed us. We had no idea it was there."

John Guest commented, "There was clearly a longing in the hearts of all the people down there that we have a school that trained leaders differently than they were then being trained. God had moved in their lives so that they said, 'Wouldn't it be wonderful if we had a school turning out leaders who were not only encouraging us in whatever God has done in our lives, but causing the same spiritual resurrection in the lives of others in the pews of Episcopal churches across the land?'"

Lynn Fairfield, who would later become part of the new school, remembers, "The whole mood of the conference was ecstatic. Everyone was hungry for fellowship. Members of the clergy were mobbed by lay people who had found no interest in renewal in their local parishes. It was as if a family whose members had never met each other suddenly had a family reunion. The standing ovation continued for a long time."

The overwhelming support of fellow believers spurred the small Board of the Fellowship of Witness on. It was time to put the plan into action.

So John Guest went home and wrote a letter.

2

Called Out of Retirement

"I have to say in all candor that unless we get a man of your caliber from somewhere in the Anglican communion, we are going to have a very difficult time," wrote John Guest. "We must enlist as our first president a man of such formidable reputation in the Anglican and evangelical world that he could draw around him a faculty which would immediately make the seminary attractive to students and a theological force to be reckoned with. Please, please make this a matter of earnest prayer."

At the urging of his friend, Anglican evangelical leader John Stott, John Guest was making this request to the Rt. Rev. Alfred Stanway, an Australian who had served in East Africa for thirty-four years, twenty of them as Bishop of Central Tanganyika.

It was as a young man of nineteen that Alfred had been converted, on Sunday the 29th of July, 1928. He was attending an evening service at his parish church, St. Paul's, Fairfield, in Melbourne, Victoria. The visiting preacher, the Rev. Mr. C.H. Nash, was preaching from Luke 12:4,5: "I tell you, my friends, do not be afraid of those who kill the body and after that can do no more. But I will show you whom you should fear: Fear him who, after the killing of the body, has power to throw you into hell. Yes, I tell you, fear him."

Alf listened intently, following Mr. Nash's argument closely, and committed his life to the Lord as a result of that sermon.

About nine months later, on Wednesday May 22, 1929, he attended an old-fashioned "lantern lecture", or slide presentation, in the Parish Hall. The handbill had caught his eye:

In Darkest Africa
The Challenge of Tanganyika
Moving Picture and Lantern Talk
by
The Rev. R.C.M. Long, B.A. Th.L
Hon. Sec. C.M.S.

Slides mostly from the camera of
the Bishop of Central Tanganyika, the
new Australian Diocese in Africa
8 p.m.

Tell others   Collection for C.M.S.   All welcome

During the talk, Alf was overcome. He couldn't sit still at all, but stood up, moving about the room, as he hung on every word. Finally, he sat down next to the Vicar and whispered, "God is calling me to Africa."

Shortly afterward, he went to the Church Missionary Society to see Mr. Long, who advised him to enter Ridley College for a three-year theology course. At the time, Alf was an accountant with a publishing company. He didn't have the necessary background to meet the College's entrance requirements. So he continued on in his job, catching up on his courses at night. He was finally able to enter Ridley in March of 1932.

These were busy years for Alf. He was ordained a deacon near the end of 1934, served as a curate in a parish for the following year, and was made a priest soon after that. At his ordination service, he placed his last two shillings in the offering plate as a symbol of his commitment to God.

Alf maintained a regular association with the Church Missionary Society during this time, particularly in the C.M.S. League of Youth. This organization had branches in local parishes, but usually met centrally in the city for weekly Bible studies for young Anglicans between the ages of fifteen and thirty.

The motto of the group was the verse from the account of the wedding at Cana: "Whatsoever He saith unto you, do it." Members had to be committed to Christ as Lord and to be willing to serve Him wherever He called, at home or overseas.

During the 1930's, Alf was the Chairman of this League of Youth. He organized regular rallies. There were hikes, and camps, and river trips during Easter and Christmas vacations. Missionaries home on leave often spoke to the young people, of whom literally dozens gave their lives to full-time service in ministry at home and abroad.

As he grew as a Christian leader, Alf learned the joy and power of prayer.

"We used to send out a prayer list of things to pray for," he recalled. "When the answers came, we'd come and tell the people that the answers had come. Those that rejoiced when the answers came were the ones that had prayed for the answers. Those who hadn't prayed didn't know anything of the joy of the answer. The joy is always with those that have prayed.

"There's a little verse in the passage about Jesus turning the water into wine. The guests at the wedding didn't know how the water had been turned into wine, but the servants who had drawn the water, they knew. The ones who did the work, they realized with joy what Jesus had done. Those who pray realize what God has done."

The economic depression of the early 1930's complicated Alf's circumstances. The Australian C.M.S. could not promise the funds to send him out immediately, so his wait continued as his papers were sent on to London.

In the meantime, he took a primary teaching course at Melbourne Teachers College. If missionaries had teaching qualifications, they could teach at Christian schools in Africa and draw their salary from the government. Several mission posts were created this way when money was tight.

And as he waited, he learned to leave things in God's hands.

"Once," he recalled, "I stayed in a parish in Sidney at the home of the Canon. He was a great man of prayer. After breakfast, we had family prayers. And I remember now that it was the first time I'd been at this sort of family prayers anywhere. And the man prayed. He prayed for his family, for the ones that were away at school and college. And he put them in God's hands, and I knew that's where they were. He prayed for the Archbishop of Sidney and put him in God's hands, and as he prayed, I had the feeling, 'That's that.' There was a kind of finality about it. He took things and people, and put them into God's hands. And he left me with the deep impression that it was because he had put them into God's hands that his prayers were answered."

Finally, Alf was accepted by the Parent Society and given his first assignment: a boys' boarding school located inland from Mombasa in Kenya. It must have been with a deep sense of gratitude and anticipation that Alf set sail from Melbourne on January 26, 1937, nearly eight years after he had first been called to Africa.

He plunged into his work immediately upon arrival in Kenya a month later. He not only taught and exercised a ministry among the boys; he also visited and supervised schools in the bush country and led Sunday services throughout the district.

Early in May 1939, his fiancee, Marjory, left Melbourne to join him. They were married in the Mombasa Memorial Cathedral on June 3.

By 1944, the Bishop of Mombasa wanted to place Alf in full-time pastoral work, so he moved him 800 miles inland, near Lake Victoria. Here Alf was responsible as Rural Dean for the oversight of three hundred and fifty churches and numerous schools, including two girls' boarding schools, a secondary boys' boarding school, and a teacher training institute.

After a time of leave in Melbourne in 1947, the Stanways returned, and were sent to Nairobi, the capital city of Kenya. There Alf was appointed Secretary of the African Education Board, with responsibility for the oversight of the Diocesan African Schools in

Kenya. In 1948, he became one of two Archdeacons of Kenya, working primarily on the African Church side of the Synod. He was also a Canon of two cathedrals, the one in Mombasa, and the other in Nairobi.

In September of 1950, the Archbishop of Canterbury called him to accept appointment as the Bishop of Central Tanganyika. On February 2, 1951, Alf was consecrated in Westminster Abbey by the Archbishop of Canterbury as the third Bishop of Central Tanganyika. At the end of the month, he flew to Nairobi and drove the four hundred and forty miles to Dodoma, where he was enthroned in the Cathedral of the Holy Spirit.

From the earliest days of his ministry in East Africa, Bishop Stanway initiated small projects and gradually built them up. He built a new leprosy center with hospital and staff houses; a complete school and chapel for blind boys; several new Bible schools; a secondary girls' boarding school; a secondary boys' school; and a three-story Diocesan headquarters, along with a bookshop, a pharmacy, and clinics for a dentist, a general practitioner, and an optician.

Everywhere he worked, he started bookshops to sell Christian literature. Drawing from his years as an accountant in a publishing firm, he worked with another missionary with similar experience to set up the Central Tanganyika Press, which now publishes for Tanzania and other countries as well.

He learned, and demonstrated repeatedly, that prayer was a crucial preliminary and accompaniment to any work of the Lord. He prayed about any new project and asked God for a "sign" for going ahead before he acted. As the money came in, he prayed for the personnel required. He found each answer to prayer to be a double blessing, for it contained not only the answer itself, but also an experience of God. And so, each answer to prayer became a preparation and encouragement towards undertaking another project in His name.

When he resigned in 1971 after twenty years as Bishop of Central Tanganyika, the number of missionaries in the Diocese had more than doubled. Increasingly, leadership positions were being filled by Africans. And in addition to the hospitals and schools, new parishes had been formed, often at the rate of two per week. At that time, he resigned from C.M.S. and returned to Australia to serve as Deputy Principal of his seminary, Ridley College in Melbourne. While he was there, the Principal, Dr. Leon Morris, asked him to represent Ridley at the meetings of the heads of all the different colleges that were part of Melbourne University. As a result, the Bishop learned what were the problems of running colleges: administrative problems, financial problems, government requirements. Though he didn't know it at the time, God was preparing him for the call that would come.

It was Bishop Stanway's routine to handle correspondence in the morning. He would read through the day's mail and pass the stack to his wife Marjory. Early in November of 1974, John Guest's letter arrived—a "'bombshell' into our home". The Stanways had had many letters over the years, encouraging them to accept a new call. But the Bishop knew that this request was not like the others.

He didn't say anything, but just slipped the letter into the middle of the pile and passed it on to his wife, believing that she would say "No". They had already lived on two continents, and had returned to Australia only a few years earlier. They were approaching retirement. He was reluctant to ask her to move again.

And from what she knew of the United States, Marjory had never cared to visit. Though the Bishop had traveled there seven or eight times, she had not accompanied him.

"He was rushed off his feet for four or five meetings every day," she said. "My impression was one of too much haste and over-organization for me to want to share that!"

But when she came to John Guest's letter in the stack, she simply said, "I think you ought to consider it, Alf."

They began to pray and ask God for guidance, committing themselves beforehand to do whatever He showed to be His will. The Bishop was moved by the great vision of this group from the

Fellowship of Witness. He responded to the letter, wanting to know more.

It turned out that he had met Peter Moore in 1962 on one of his earlier journeys to the United States. Later he said, "He was one of the first two Americans I put on my prayer list. I've had him there ever since. I've been associated with him in different ways in the time in between, and when I found out that Peter was to be the Chairman of the Board, I realized that is one of the reasons why God had me pray for him long ago. I recognized the gifts that God had given him, and I realized the potential that was in him. How wonderful it is to look back and see that particular fact, and I am grateful to God for it."

Bishop Stanway also turned to his old friends for advice, Sir Marcus Loane and the Rev. Dr. John Stott. He learned that it had been John Stott who had put his name before the Americans. He thought maybe he had just mentioned it in passing. But John wrote him a letter which convinced him, encouraging him to accept the offer.

As he reflected on his four short years at Ridley, he began to feel that he had made his major contribution there. He had re-organized the administration in such a way that he could pass the work on to a successor. And he realized that God had given him those four years so that he could learn about how to lead colleges. So while he probably wouldn't have resigned if no invitation had come, when the invitation did come, he felt at peace about leaving Ridley to accept the new call.

Marjory later said, "During our lives together, the peace of God had become the factor which always determined whether we said 'yes' or 'no' to a proposition. I let Alf make the decision, saying that if God made it clear that it was right for him, then I knew it would be right for me. When he decided to accept, I had peace in my heart about going."

3

This Is of God

A few months after receiving John Guest's letter, Bishop Stanway traveled to the United States to visit with the Fellowship of Witness, and was impressed with what he saw. Over the course of the spring of 1975, he felt that this call was of God, and agreed to pursue it.

In May, he came over again to meet with the pro tem committee of the Fellowship of Witness. A small Board of Trustees was formed for the School, including John Guest, Peter Moore, and Bishop Stanway. The group's first official decision was to call Alfred Stanway to be the first President of Trinity Episcopal School for Ministry. It was decided that he would begin employment in September of that year.

Bishop Stanway soon proved to be an inspiration to the Board. He made it clear that the best way to implement such a great vision was to begin small. He was confident that God would show them what steps to take as they prayed. As they were faithful to what He was telling them, He would continue to guide and lead them. The School would grow and thrive, as long as they were concerned with His glory, through the making known of Christ.

He warned that not one of them, including he himself, was capable of seeing the whole vision right from the beginning. He knew from experience that God very seldom gives such a large task to one person to carry through on his own. Instead, they would need to work together, seeking by prayer to involve the right leadership, diligently pursuing the project as God showed them.

So the Board began to tackle the components of a good school one by one. For the present, money was not a pressing concern. But the prime donor's gift would be quickly used up. Then where would money come from? How much would be needed to open the School?

The question of location was of primary importance. A classroom and some office space would be needed for the first year. Married students and their families would have to find local housing, but the School would probably need to provide dormitories for single students. Eventually, there would have to be a chapel, a library, more classrooms, more offices. Should the Board continue to look for buildings to rent, or should it explore the purchase of land?

What about a library? Thousands of volumes would eventually be needed. Some would inevitably be donated but many more would have to be bought. And until a permanent site were found, they would have to be stored. Was there any way in which library facilities could be arranged for the early students before Trinity could build up its own?

Accreditation in the Commonwealth of Pennsylvania required three full-time teachers, in addition to the administrative staff. Where would these faculty members come from? It was essential to have teachers who would uphold the authority of Scripture. At the same time, it was important to find scholars who affirmed the Anglican tradition. After all, this was to be an Episcopal school.

Similarly, the Board needed additional members. But it was important to find people who concurred with this vision. Otherwise, individuals could be appointed to the Board who disagreed in some small way with the original concept, but who had so much going for them in other ways that they were allowed to stay. Gradually, others would come along who differed a little more. Soon the School would have drifted away from the intentions of its founders. Maybe there should be a statement of faith that Board members would have to sign. Otherwise, where would Trinity be theologically in fifteen years?

It was important to build good public relations. The new School needed to be made known in a positive way. Who were the key people to be notified of the school's official creation?

As these founders discussed and prayed over the work to be done, they asked God to show them how to begin.

They brainstormed names of potential faculty members for Bishop Stanway to consider.

They authorized John Guest to continue exploring buildings to be leased or purchased.

They put another member in charge of developing a logo, some stationery, and other promotional material.

They suggested asking FOW members to set aside five books to donate to the library.

They tossed around names for potential Board members: other clergy; educators; people from business and professional fields.

By the end of their time together, each person had several assignments to pursue before they would meet again in October. In the meantime, they were to work, to pass the word, and especially to pray. They prayed that God would help them to get the school going and would continue to confirm to them that they were on the right track.

He was not slow in answering!

Bishop Stanway felt it was crucial that he be accepted into the Diocese of Pittsburgh by the diocesan bishop, Robert Appleyard. It was so important to him that he made this acceptance one of the conditions on which he would come to the United States.

A few days after the Board meeting, he did go in to Pittsburgh to visit Bishop Appleyard. Bishop Appleyard knew of Bishop Stanway's reputation, his twenty years as Bishop of Central Tanganyika, his leadership among evangelicals. He was confident that, with years of experience, Bishop Stanway knew the problems inherent in starting a new work: the lack of finances, of staff, of support from key leaders in the Church.

He was also encouraged as Bishop Stanway described the School to him as a school for ministry, where leaders would be trained to equip others to exercise their ministries, and where all people could come to learn. He was reassured by Bishop Stanway's approach of starting small with a tiny, but good, faculty. And he agreed that the School, though welcomed into relationship with the diocese, should be a separate institution.

"I still felt that this was a risk," said Bishop Appleyard, "but this is what Christian faith is all about, taking risks."

For his part, Bishop Stanway saw this reception as an answer to prayer and as another confirming sign that it was God's plan for him to come to Trinity.

It just so happened that, during this same period of time, Les and Lynn Fairfield stopped in Sewickley on their way from Indiana to New England to visit family. Lynn had attended the conference in Atlanta the previous fall and had returned home elated about the news of a new school starting.

Meanwhile, Les, who had been teaching history at Purdue, had begun to explore the possibility of a call to ordained ministry. He was also entertaining the idea of teaching at the new School. So he wrote to the Board of the Fellowship of Witness, sending his resume.

"I got an appointment with John Guest," he remembered, "and it turned out that Bishop Stanway was there also. The Bishop wasn't certain that they could afford a church historian in the first year, but they did interview me, and the Bishop wanted to meet Lynn.

"We walked together down the narrow sidewalk along the highway to the Holiday Inn. He was talking quite excitedly about the new school, but the traffic was roaring past, and he was walking so briskly, I could barely hear him. But I was glad that he wanted to meet my wife and to know all about her relationship with Christ."

And the Board members saw Les's interest as another confirmation that God was leading them. John Guest reflected, "Here was a man who was teaching at Purdue; he had his doctorate from Harvard. When someone with a position like that has heard that you're starting a new school and wants to see you about it, it's pretty encouraging!"

Wednesday was the last day of Bishop Stanway's trip. His plane for Australia was due to leave that afternoon.

That morning, Kathie Guest, John's wife, happened to be at a meeting for mothers of kindergarten children. In the course of conversation, someone mentioned that the little house on Henry Avenue was for sale. There would be an Open House on Friday.

Kathie had always admired that house. It seemed so inviting to her whenever she saw it from the church parking lot. She wondered what it was like inside.

Later that same morning, she took her daughter down to the church to play with a friend. As she was returning to her car, she just happened to look up Henry Avenue, and saw a woman unlocking the door of number 341. Out of curiosity, she walked over and knocked. She explained that Bishop Stanway would be moving from Australia to Sewickley to start a school for ministry, and that he would need a place to live. She asked if she could see the house.

The woman agreed. She didn't live there; she had just inherited the house. But she would be around for a little while, waiting for a washer and dryer to be delivered.

As Kathie walked from room to room, she remembered the list of things the Bishop had said he would need in a house. There were the four bedrooms.

"Four bedrooms?" Kathie had asked, wondering why the Stanways would need all that space for just the two of them.

"Yes," he had answered. "When you're starting a new work, you can expect many overnight guests. One larger bedroom for couples, a smaller one for singles, one for an office, and the other for us."

It also had to be clean.

"Clean?", Kathie remembered. "That house was spotless. It was in such good condition that even the basement was painted!"

And of course, the location was ideal. Living a block from St. Stephen's, the Stanways would be part of the fellowship of that growing, Bible-centered parish.

Kathie thanked the woman and asked if she could return with the Bishop. Again the woman agreed.

Kathie quickly telephoned the Bishop at the Chalfants' home where he was packing his suitcase. He was interested, and walked through the house with her an hour later. He confirmed that it was well suited to their needs. If the Board felt that it was right, he and Marjory would be glad to live there. And with that, he was on his way home to Australia.

Later that same day, Kathie brought her husband John to the house. The more she saw it, the more "right" it seemed.

The next day, John checked the listed price and prepared to make a lower offer. But a lawyer from the parish cautioned him that the owner's price was reasonable. Unless John offered her the full amount, someone viewing the property at the Open House would make a higher offer than his.

John thought it over and called the woman back on Thursday night, offering the amount she was asking. She went ahead with the Open House on Friday, but as soon as it was over, she closed the front door, called John, and accepted his offer.

"It was amazing," Kathie said, her clear blue eyes alight with the memory. "The house was for sale at just the right time, and the price was so affordable. The Board even had to insure the house for more than what it ended up paying for it!

"And God must have opened the woman's heart. I think she really wanted the Bishop to have it. It was a clear encouragement to all of us."

The only other immediate need was a good secretary.

It just so happened that one of the secretaries at St. Stephen's, Betty Buckingham, had come to Sewickley a few years earlier at the request of John Howe. She had worked a number of years at InterVarsity in Philadelphia, and then with the Latin American Mission in Costa Rica.

As she typed letters for John Guest and the Fellowship of Witness, Betty was excited about this missionary vision. So when Bishop Stanway wrote, asking her to work for the new School, she responded eagerly; as she thought about all she had learned while working in the church, and about the people she had come to know, and about her own missionary background, she realized she could be helpful to Bishop Stanway. Maybe this was why God had brought her to Pittsburgh, she thought.

And so, Bishop Stanway left Australia in September, on his 67th birthday, and moved to Sewickley. For the first few weeks, when he "went to the office", it was to Betty Buckingham's living room, where she kept the two cardboard boxes of file folders that constituted Trinity Episcopal School for Ministry!

4

Implementing the Vision

I t turned out to be easy to get interested people together to serve on the Board of Trustees for Trinity Episcopal School for Ministry. Eighteen members gathered at Grace Church in New York City on October 8, 1975. The first meeting was held in conjunction with the National Renewal Conference, similar to the one in Atlanta at which John Guest had announced the new school only a year before.

The Rev. James Hampson did much of the work on drafting a Statement of Faith (see Appendix), working in consultation with theologians John Stott and J.I. Packer. This foundational document was to be crucial in defining Trinity, and in helping to articulate the School's vision. Board members, and later, faculty and graduating seniors would all be asked to sign it.

John Guest had been pursuing possible locations for the new School. A rehabilitation home, an apartment complex, and a motel had been considered, but all fell through.

Then suddenly a new option came up. Trinity might be able to rent space at Robert Morris College, just across the Ohio River from Sewickley. The School could lease dorm space for up to 44 students, a classroom with an office next to it, and the use of all other college facilities. The Rev. Rodgers Wood, rector of St. Philip's Church in Moon Township, where Robert Morris was located, was open to letting Trinity use the church building for school-wide fellowship and worship one evening per week.

The Board voted unanimously to move forward with arrangements at the College. Meanwhile, the Bishop asked the Trustees to think ahead about buying land. He hoped large bequests would make this possible.

Another important issue was how to go about promoting the School. In October, the Bishop spoke of a "Community of Interest"; he hoped, and was praying for, at least 2,000 people who would be committed to giving annually. The School needed both one-time givers and sustainers. The Board members each committed to recruiting individuals for this Community of Interest, and to raising a certain amount of money.

The initial criticism the Board faced was that, with all the seminaries having such a hard time financially, a new school would just siphon off students and money from the others, which were already struggling. Many in the Church felt that there should be fewer seminaries, not more.

Trinity was also perceived as a threat theologically, not just financially. The very fact that it was coming into existence was a statement of criticism, because it implied that the other schools were not doing a good job. But the Board members were unanimous in being positive about TESM without being critical about other seminaries.

So Bishop Stanway cautioned the Board not to run ahead of the Lord. Too much publicity, "too hard a sell", would make it seem as though they were trying to take money away from other seminaries. Then bishops who may have already had vague fears that the School would be narrowly "fundamentalist", would be forced to take a stand, one that would most likely be negative. And the School would have the large and unpleasant job of having to change people's minds.

Spiritual Principles

As these Christians gathered to face such major concerns in the early stages of the School's life, they began to grow spiritually as the task before them seemed too great. It was a time that called for both prayer and action, both listening for the Lord's guidance and putting into practice what He showed to be His will.

During his years with the Church Missionary Society, Bishop Stanway had adopted the C.M.S. Principles. He had lived and led by them for so many years that he naturally continued to do so. He challenged the Board members to:

a) Start small, even while intending great things,
b) Follow the leading of God,
c) Put money in a secondary place, and
d) Choose fellow workers through prayer, saying "Under God, everything depends on the quality of the people chosen for the task."

God had certainly given these founders an extravagant vision of a new school for ministry in the Episcopal Church. They hoped to train graduates whose leadership would eventually turn around a denomination which was straying farther and farther away from an understanding of the Scriptures as the authority for doctrine and life.

But while the Trustees had to keep that goal in mind, and pray and work toward it, they also had to start somewhere. Rented facilities—no faculty members—a very small Community of Interest—and an uncertain number of students—it was an inauspicious start. But it was a start nonetheless. It was something.

If they waited until they could start even a medium-sized school, they might never begin. But it would take courage to hold on to a large vision in the midst of small circumstances.

When the Bishop urged the Board members to follow the leading of God, he was issuing a call to prayer. He believed it was possible to know the will of God in most things, citing Ephesians 5:17: "Do not be foolish, but understand what the Lord's will is." In fact, he felt it was imperative to spend time discovering what was the will of God.

"The danger in projects is thinking before praying. It's likely to happen because we get attached to our own ideas quite easily. But if you pray last, you get nowhere fast! Prayer is important in every step, even when you know the project is right.

"Half the problem is that we think we know what we ought to do. We've got it all quite clear-cut, and we want the Lord to work it just according to our plan. We want Him to do this, and then this, and then this, and then this, and then we'll call that 'blessed'.

That isn't the way it works out at all. You're in business when you say to the Lord, 'We don't know what we ought to do. We lift our eyes to Thee.'

"And then, when God gives you guidance, it's meant to be followed. In fact, you can't go to Him for guidance unless you're prepared to be obedient to the guidance you receive. So ask with assurance, expecting the next thing next, committing your hearts and minds to do whatever He shows to be His will.

"He will speak to you, not in a voice, but in an inner conviction, audible to the inner ear. If you obey what He tells you, He'll never stop speaking to you. Spiritual hearing is increased by use."

Bishop Stanway continually stressed the need to keep money from being the dominant basis or the limit to what the School could be and do: "It's a very good thing, whenever you're praying for money, to get it quite clear in your mind that God is not short of money. He's got it all. Bankers think **they** have it. Rich men think **they** have it. In actual fact, 'the silver is mine, saith the Lord of hosts'. And He can have it all, all He wants, when He requires it. He can meet every need. So have faith that God will provide, because with Him there is no shortage.

"And avoid extravagance. The right use of money given is the best guarantee of a fresh supply. Money will always be available if we are in the will of God."

God Is Able

Bishop Stanway himself had to remember all that he'd learned in his walk with God. While his encouragement and leadership spurred the Board members on to greater faith, he sometimes needed to remind himself to trust more fully in God's ability to provide.

He often commented, though without complaining, that starting up this School was the hardest task he'd ever had. At one stage during the fall of 1975, when there were no other staff, no faculty, no buildings, no students, no bishops openly supporting the school, he began to think back to his days in Tanganyika.

He reflected, "When we needed land and property, God gave us land and property. We needed qualified staff; God gave us qualified staff. We needed money; God gave us money. I found in my past experience—everything that we required had happened to me previously in my life, and in great measure. How then could I doubt that God was able to do it now, just because it was a different land, and a different country, and different people? God is able—I didn't have to ask myself the question, '**Can** God...?"

When he had wanted to rebuild the Mvumi Hospital in Africa, he had prayed for many months about it, because he knew it would require a lot of money. At one point, he went to an ecumenical conference in Nairobi, where he shared a cubicle with an elderly German gentleman. They got to talking to one another, and Bishop Stanway asked him what he was doing at the conference.

"I've come to represent Bread for the World."

"What's that?"

"Well, in West Germany, we take up an offering in all the churches once a year, and we give it for work outside of Germany, especially in the developing nations."

"What kind of work?"

"Oh, schools and hospitals..."

"Hospitals?"

"Do you have a hospital that needs help?"

"Very much so." And Bishop Stanway began to tell him about the hospital.

"What do you need? 50,000 pounds or 100,000 pounds?"

"Well, 100,000 pounds would be good!"

In the end it turned out to be close to 200,000 pounds. The bishop had waited and prayed for nearly two years, and when the time was right, God provided dramatically. Two new wards were built, and a new operating room, and the hospital was turned around.

Another time, Ken Short, a missionary under Bishop Stanway, felt that God was calling him to double the size of the church. So the congregation prayed and set a "day of gifts" to get the money that was required.

In that area, there was a district commissioner, who didn't really believe in what he called "this faith business". He believed in "practical politics". When Ken visited him in one of the branch churches, he said, "I'll give you my check. It's signed, and the amount isn't filled in. When you find out how much you're short on the day of gifts, you can fill it in for the balance."

Ken said, "I will take your check because I haven't got the right to refuse it, but let me tell you now in the name of the Lord, that it will never need to be filled in, because you don't believe that God can meet the need. But He'll meet it without your check, so that you may know that He **can** meet the need."

And sure enough! Ken and others prayed, and God provided all that was needed. When the commissioner filled in the check afterwards as an extra gift, he'd learned his lesson! He thought he could make up what God didn't provide, and God doesn't act that way.

100 Pounds In Christchurch

Many times, the Lord had worked through Bishop Stanway to teach others that He was able to provide all that was needed. Once, he stayed with the bishop of Christchurch in New Zealand. As they were talking about faith and various other things, Bishop Stanway told the man what had happened when he first became bishop in Tanganyika: someone had warned him that people didn't give as generously as they used to. In the former days, bishops used to preach, and individuals would respond by donating as much as a hundred pounds to the work of God.

"Absolute nonsense!" Bishop Stanway had responded. "People still buy refrigerators, and go on world trips. There must still be some people who've got a hundred pounds to give away."

He went off to preach the next Sunday morning, and, though he never appealed for any money, a woman approached him after the service because she wanted to give him a hundred pounds for the Church in Tanganyika!

The next day, the Bishop saw at the Church Missionary Society headquarters the man who had warned him, and told him, "Well, the Lord did provide a hundred pounds!"

Three days later, he saw the man again, and showed him another letter he'd received with an extra check inside for a hundred pounds.

"You already told me about that," replied the man.

"No, that was Sunday. This just came in the mail."

"Well, what did you say?"

"I didn't say anything—I didn't ask for any money at all. You said there weren't people whom God could get to give a hundred pounds—it isn't true!"

As Bishop Stanway told this story to the bishop of Christchurch, that bishop's son, who was about to begin his training for the ministry, said, "You can't do it in Christchurch."

Bishop Stanway's response was quick. "God can do it anywhere."

"I still don't think it could happen here."

"God can do it anywhere," Bishop Stanway insisted. "I'll tell you what I'll do. I won't make any appeals for money on Sunday. But I will ask God to raise a hundred pounds for Tanganyika on Sunday, so that you might know that God **can** provide a hundred pounds in Christchurch."

When Sunday morning came, the man who was supposed to drive Bishop Stanway around to various churches was unable to do so. Someone else volunteered, a businessman. As they drove, he and the bishop got to talking about "capturing the initiative" in business. As they pulled up to the church, the man said, "I'll give you seventy-five pounds to 'capture the initiative' in Tanganyika!" The Lord had already provided three quarters of the amount, and Bishop Stanway hadn't even started to preach!

After the service, a lady gave him five pounds as she was going out the door. He spoke at several other churches that afternoon, but never stayed long enough for people to give him any money.

At the end of the last service, the vicar said to him, "Well, you know, we give to Melanesia, so we can't really give to Tanganyika, and things aren't all that good at the moment, but thank you very much for coming. Let's go across to the hall and get some coffee."

In the parish hall, one of the church wardens came up to them and said, "Vicar, we were looking for you and couldn't find you. We just had a little meeting of the church wardens and vestrymen. We've decided to give the Bishop twenty pounds for Tanganyika!"

So there was the hundred pounds!

Five years later, Bishop Stanway was riding along the same road and remembered God's earlier provision. He leaned back in his seat and silently thanked the Lord for the hundred pounds that He had given in answer to prayer. Just then, the driver of the car turned around and said to him, "Bishop, I'd like to give you a hundred pounds for Tanganyika!"

Learning To Trust

Over and over again, Bishop Stanway had experienced God's provision in unmistakable ways. And so, as he reminded himself of how the Lord had worked in the past, he taught the Board about God—His trustworthiness, His power, His resources, His desire for His people to rely on Him.

"Christians are always trying to get themselves to the place where they don't have to trust. They'd like to be sure the house is paid for, and that they've got a decent bank balance. Then they won't have to trust any more.

"And they want a good secure job. They're always looking to get to a place of security. And God is always trying to push the Christian into a place where his trust has got to be in Him. 'Without faith it is impossible to please God.'

"The same thing is true of institutions. People like large endowments—then they think the work is secure for many years. Endowments—you've got to have them sometimes. In Pennsylvania, they demand that we have one. If it wasn't for that, I wouldn't want one at all. Endowment is a method by which you keep things alive after they're dead. What you want is a living work.

"You'll find in your Christian life how grateful you are when you think you don't have to trust any more. But if you look back across your life, you'll find that the great times of blessing were when you **had** to trust, when God pushed you out on a limb. When you get an answer to your prayer, you don't just get what you trusted God for; you get an experience of God's love and God's grace and God's power. And that's worth more to you than the answer to your prayer.

"When we're looking at our need, we have to go back to the fact that the silver and the gold belong to God. There's no shortage of money with God. There never has been, and never will be. If we keep looking at our need all the time, it will seem impossible. That's too vast a sum to give. But if we look back on our past experience, if we look at God's resources, it's a different story.

"What kind of a God do you think you go to when you go to Him in prayer? How vast are His resources? He's got people everywhere that will do His will. He's got people who've got money that, if God tells them to send a check to someone, they'll get right around to it and do it straight away.

The Blessing Of Giving

"Many years ago, I was at a convention in Australia, and an old man, who happened to be the man under whom I was converted, stood up to address the convention. He said he felt there was a 'controversy' between the convention and God. They had a debt of a hundred pounds.

"He said, 'Let me tell you that most of the members of the council think we have an extension of a couple of days' time and it will do to pay it then. It should be paid now. We haven't given any notice of offerings' (and these were the days when money was not plentiful—the 1920's), 'but each of you ask God to show you what to give, and pass it along to the end of the row, and we'll take up a collection.'

"And he prayed, and asked God to show people what to give. The collection was taken up, and it came to exactly one hundred pounds!

"On the walk back, a girl said to me, 'I'm worried.'

"'What are you worried for?'

"'I've always put threepence in the collection. When I asked God how much I should give, He said, 'Three shillings.' I gave my three shillings—that's a lot for me. But if I hadn't given that three shillings, that man's prayer wouldn't have been answered!'

"I said, 'No, that isn't true. God would have found somebody less able, but more willing, to provide. And the prayer would have been answered just the same. If we don't respond when God calls us to respond, He finds somebody else. We still have the money we didn't send; **they** have the blessing we might have had.'"

He went on, "So we need to remember that God is able. We also know that those who give will receive blessing from Him.

"But when we're seeking to get people to give money for God's cause," he cautioned, "we've got to be more concerned with their spiritual growth and development than with the amount of money we get. That will stop us from trying to get it in the wrong way."

Money Follows Ministry

Bishop Stanway firmly believed that "money follows ministry". He felt that if there was a vision that God had given, then the money was assured. But that money would usually come from people who had received real ministry. They would have responded to the gospel and to God's grace working in their lives in such a way that they were open to giving of their money as they perceived God was leading.

Good stewardship happens when people who love God want to support and identify with a ministry that honors Him. Their money follows their hearts. When they see that a minister is not just after their wallets, they will give.

Certainly this idea had already proven to be true with Mrs. Chalfant's gift. She had given in response to the ministry she had received from the Lord through John Guest and St. Stephen's Church. Other money, no matter the size of the gift, should come in the same way.

So Bishop Stanway spoke at twenty-nine different churches and educational institutions in eleven dioceses in nine different states before the school even opened! The Board members, and later the faculty also, received many invitations to lead parish renewal weekends. They committed themselves to traveling and speaking to churches, not as fund-raisers per se, but as ministers of the gospel.

They shared the Good News of Christ's death and resurrection. They told of their firsthand experiences that the mighty God of the Scriptures was still at work in the lives of His people. They shared the vision of a school which would train graduates to think, and preach, and serve in a way that was faithful to the Scriptures. Without being pushy, they invited parishes and individuals to join Trinity's mailing list.

And of course, they prayed.

Once the Stanways were settled, Betty Buckingham's office was established in the pink corner bedroom upstairs. She and the Stanways would pray together daily for the church in general, for the Board members, and for God's provision of the money, and the faculty, and the students for the new school to begin.

And they watched for what the Stanways called a "harbinger". In Australia, there is a tiny flower which blooms in the late winter. It's a "harbinger" of spring, a forerunner of all the rest of the flowers. It had been the Stanways' practice for many years, with each new venture, to ask God for a "harbinger" that would show that it was right to continue on with the project.

They didn't have to wait long. One day, as Betty was in the office answering mail, a local businessman from St. Stephen's sent over a year-old IBM Selectric typewriter donated from his company. It was a small answer to prayer, but it was followed by many more.

As God moved among His people, individuals and parishes responded to the ministry of the Word, and money trickled in. It never seemed to be a stream, but it was always just enough to pay the bills and bring encouragement. In addition to the prime gift, over $60,000 was donated in 1975, so the cost of the Stanways' house was covered by those smaller contributions. By year's end, a modest car was purchased for the Bishop's use. By April of 1976, the number of donors had risen to 141. And when the school opened in September, the budget for the year had been set at $125,000. All expenses so far had been met by contributions.

This active reliance on God to supply the money at just the time when it was needed was a challenging new step of faith for many of the Board members. One man, who had recently retired from an upper-level management position, had never been part of any venture that didn't need money. On more than one occasion in the life of Trinity, an increase in spending had been approved, even though the money wasn't there. It seemed to this man a frivolous way to do business; but the Bishop always said, "I don't know what we're worrying about—God has plenty of money!" And of course, the money always came in at the last minute.

In Bishop Stanway's mind, the corollary to the abundance of God's provision was the responsibility of Trinity to use wisely the money that was given. He himself was a careful steward of both time and money, recognizing the need for equipment and facilities of high quality, but refusing to tolerate extravagance.

And it was through this combination of God's continuing financial provision and the commitment of the school to leanness of operation that Board members, working closely with the funds, saw God's hand at work most dramatically.

This commitment to faithful stewardship would become an integral part of the students' spiritual formation and preparation for ministry. From the beginning, many of Trinity's students were married, and, in most cases, those families included children. Often, personal funds would be tight. But the Bishop would advise students not to tell anyone but God of their need.

Invariably, the problem would be eased or completely taken care of within a few days. And whether it was a check in the mailbox, or free medical care, or winter coats for the children, the solutions were so varied and creative and appropriate that only a loving heavenly Father could have orchestrated them.

As individuals, the people who gathered to become part of Trinity learned over and over again, **as they prayed**, that God is sovereign, and will take care of His people. And as an institution, the School demonstrated from the beginning the truth of the principle that "God's work done in God's way shall not lack God's support."

5
Choosing Fellow Workers Through Prayer

Bishop Stanway was convinced that the selection of faculty and students was far more important than money. "If we have the right faculty and the right students, we will get the money we need. Under God, everything depends on the quality of the people chosen for the task."

He challenged the Board members to pray about the faculty appointments. So, throughout the fall of 1975, they asked God to guide them—and as they prayed, they gathered names. As they discussed potential candidates, weighing them against each other, and trusting God to work through their deliberations to make it clear whom He was calling to teach at the new school, they came around again and again to just a few names.

The Bishop was concerned that the faculty members must be people who really wanted to be teaching at Trinity, people with a strong sense of call. Top-notch professors would make bishops more receptive to ordaining the School's graduates.

By early January, Bishop Stanway was ready to talk to John Rodgers.

"When he telephoned me at home in Virginia," reflected John, "and asked if he and Marjory could come see my wife Blanche and me about exploring a call to this new seminary, it was quite a shock. Blanche took the call and, true to her name, she blanched! I was tenured at Virginia Theological Seminary (VTS), and we were there for the long haul. We're both 'nesters', and we were threatened by the thought of leaving that security. I'm the type of person who likes good ruts!"

John was committed to linking with the new school, but he had not contemplated going to it and being part of it. He had hoped to have an impact on the Episcopal Church through the existing seminaries.

He had grown up in an orthodox Presbyterian family in suburban St. Louis. By his own account, he went to church often as a child, and took the Bible and faith very seriously, treasuring the importance of Reformation emphases.

When he reached high school, he began attending worship at the local Episcopal Church because his friends went there. He found the tradition and the dignity of the service attractive, and he admired the leadership of the Rector, the Rev. Charles Kean.

After graduation, John entered the Naval Academy. That school's traditions were English, and so corporate worship followed the Prayer Book, though in simplified form. It was during these years that John became an Episcopalian and began to sense a call to seminary.

"I noticed that the Thirty-nine Articles of the Episcopal Church were similar in theological thrust to the Shorter Catechism that I had grown up with. I just assumed that all Episcopalians believed the Articles and the Prayer Book."

A few years after graduation from the Naval Academy, he enrolled at VTS. "I chose Virginia because it seemed to me to combine an emphasis on Scripture with strong pastoral concerns. I was excited by reading the Bible and by studying the lives and work of the Reformers. And my own theology began to take on a strong evangelical thrust."

After graduation from seminary, John went to work for a few years at Church of the Epiphany in Washington, D.C. He served there under the same Rev. Charles Kean whom he had known in Missouri!

"As I worked in parish ministry under this gospel-centered man, I began to see the need in our churches for a more profound grasp of Biblical doctrine. We also had to find a way of relating the gospel to ministry so people's lives could be more decisively claimed for Christ. I was aware of the contrast between our increasingly secular society on the one hand, and Biblical doctrine and ethics on the other."

This concern for doctrine, coupled with the gift for teaching that others had helped him identify while he was in seminary, led John to consider seeking a doctorate. So in 1960, he and his new wife Blanche headed to Switzerland, choosing to study at the University of Basel. He looked forward to learning from Karl Barth—John called him the "best doctrine man"—because of the renowned theologian's deliberate approach of letting theology come out of the Bible. Other excellent teaching was to come from Oscar Cullman on the New Testament and from Walter Eichrodt on the Old Testament.

"After I had determined what God was calling me to do, I applied for money to all who were giving it away. Once I had all the funds in hand, I committed myself to going to Basel. I've done things a little differently since I met Alf Stanway!"

The Rodgers stayed at Basel for three years, where John wrote and published his dissertation on P.T. Forsyth. Both Forsyth and Martin Luther became great heroes in theology for John, because they had been theologians involved in powerful spiritual renewal in the practice of ministry.

He returned to the United States in 1963 to teach at Virginia as an assistant professor in systematic theology. As the years passed, he moved on up the ladder, becoming an associate professor, then a tenured professor, the head of the department, chaplain, and eventually associate dean of students.

"When I first returned, I found the "God-is-dead" movement to be very significant. Now that phrase is a pathetic theological statement, but it clearly showed the anchorlessness and bankruptcy of theology apart from Scripture. It chases after 'something to believe in, something relevant' rather than starting with the Biblical revelation of Someone, and then building around that. As a reaction, I became committed to the conviction that the content of God's revelation is contained in Scripture, God's Word written."

During these early years at VTS, John began to meet and enter into fellowship with Philip Hughes, Peter Moore, and a number of other evangelicals in the Church. He participated in a key conference of the Fellowship of Witness at St. James' Church in

Leesburg, Virginia in 1968. John Stott also attended, and the two began a "long and happy relationship".

But John was particularly challenged by Philip Hughes. "He was clearly concerned with calling people to repentance and faith, and he gave me the courage to do that, too. As the secularity of the culture increased, it was becoming essential for Christians to issue a call to clear commitment."

During this time, John also met John Guest. "I had come to Sewickley for the Fellowship of Witness before, and I found John to be challenging, and his work going well. Together, he and John Howe began to lead all of us in FOW beyond merely being a gathering of like-minded people to the point where we worked to commend the faith and not just to maintain it.

"John and I chatted some about the seminaries. He felt strongly that the schools were too little Biblical in both theology and practice. According to him, there was too much maintenance, and too little missions. My primary concern was that seminaries needed to have a strong view of the authority of Scripture, and that we evangelicals needed to wrestle with the place of critical tools in all of that.

"But I was content to remain at Virginia. During the sixties, we had started a Bible Study in our home following the Wednesday evening Eucharist. Over the years, the group grew, if only because Virginia was attracting more students who had had a background in InterVarsity or Faith Alive. I just assumed that God had called me to be the faculty link with that group until I retired."

So Bishop Stanway's telephone call was very threatening. But he and Marjory went down to see the Rodgers in January of 1976. Blanche showed them into the study, and then she had to leave. And she was quite pleased that she had to pick up their son Paul at nursery school. She didn't want to talk with the Stanways. She was hoping the whole subject would go away!

She went over to the school, only to find that Paul had gone home for lunch with a friend. With time on her hands, but wanting to avoid the discussion taking place at the house, she decided to stop in at the Roy Rogers restaurant for some lunch, hoping for anonymity and a place to sit by herself and think.

The Rodgers had lived in Alexandria for thirteen years, and she had never been in that restaurant. But when she walked in, there they were—the Bishop, Marjory, and John—and of course, she had to sit with them, listening to the proposal and the dream.

John kept trying to raise objections to the Bishop. He observed that, while Mrs. Chalfant's gift was a lot of money, it wouldn't go far or last long. With his family of six, he would be too costly. It would be more prudent for the school to hire a single man.

In his characteristically abrupt way, Bishop Stanway said that that was up to the Board. John's task was to discern whether or not God was calling him through TESM's invitation.

John commented, "Now Alf didn't realize that American theology is very Deistic. We believe in God and the Scriptures, but we tend to see Him as more distant—as the Creator and Redeemer, but not generally involved in day-to-day affairs."

So John asked, "How can I accept such a call and place my wife and children in such a shakily financed venture?"

The Bishop's reply was quick, "Do you believe God loves your wife and children?"

"Well, yes."

"If He's calling you, isn't He committing Himself to provide for your wife and your children?"

"Well, that is what Christ teaches, but we've never lived that way."

"Maybe it's time to start!"

With that, the Stanways began to speak in sequential logic about the work of the mighty and loving Father in and through His children's lives. They told tale after tale from their own experience of God's provision for them on the mission field.

Later, John reflected, "I knew that Alf had grown up in the tail end of the Victorian era. I knew he wouldn't exaggerate. And yet, as he described twentieth century Africa to us, it sounded like the book of Acts. And because they had witnessed what they were talking about, I couldn't deny it or dismiss it."

The meeting ended with Bishop Stanway asking, "If God were to call you, would you come?"

"Well, of course I would," John responded. "What choice would I have?"

The Stanways smiled and went back to Sewickley, leaving John with a wife who wouldn't talk to him.

The Bishop reported back to the Board, giving a very warm endorsement of John. He believed him to be the kind of man with whom he could work. His recent visit to Alexandria had convinced him that John would come if he were invited to occupy the top teaching post. He would be an excellent leader of small seminars, and proficient at building personal relationships with students. He might even fill a future role as academic dean. Certainly, Episcopal bishops would have confidence in him when it came to the question of ordaining Trinity graduates.

Meanwhile, the Rodgers weren't so sure. They began to weigh all the considerations, and to pray for God to make His way known to them. They appreciated the fact that Bishop Stanway hadn't pressured them, but had left it up to God to call them.

As the question arose of whether or not to leave VTS, John tried to measure where he might have the greatest effectiveness in helping to lead the Church in renewal. He looked at recent voting in the General Conventions and noted that the laity had increasingly voted according to Scriptural principles on decisions, while the clergy were doing so less and less.

"I asked myself, 'What are clergy but laity who have gone to school?' And I began to see more clearly that the problem was with the schools. Maybe it would be best to come to Trinity, and be part of starting a completely new school."

As he became more open to the idea of accepting the call, he wanted to be careful not to force Blanche. He began to pray that God would get the word to her if He wanted them to go.

After a few weeks, they had no clear leading, but accepted an invitation from the Stanways to visit Sewickley. They were picked up at the airport and driven the ten minutes to St. Stephen's Church where they were to meet with John Guest and the Bishop.

Blanche still had strong reservations about this calling; she had a splitting headache, and did not feel like talking to her husband.

So she browsed through the rack of books for sale, and picked out a small one by Festo Kivengere, an Anglican bishop in Uganda. As she sat and read the first few chapters, she had a strong sense of the Lord breaking down her fears and making them vanish.

Later that same day, the Rodgers had lunch with John and Susan Yates. John was one of the assistant rectors at St. Stephen's, and had jumped at the opportunity to get to know the Stanways and learn from them. As he and Susan shared so positively about the Bishop and his leadership and the great vision, John and Blanche were each warming to the idea more and more.

Independently of each other, they both concluded that God was calling them to Sewickley. Blanche went back to Alexandria a day ahead of John. She recalls the moment she knew it was OK: as she looked out the window of the plane, she saw her reflection. It was a smile—for the first time in a month!

They returned to VTS, and told everyone that God had called them to this new venture. They wept and prayed with their many friends. It would be hard to leave them.

A few weeks later, the whole family drove up to Pennsylvania for a visit. Bishop Stanway directed them to the Chalfants' home, where they were to stay. Both Chalfants were away that evening, so the Rodgers settled in on their own.

When morning came, they meandered through the house to find the kitchen. Nancy was there to make them breakfast. She was curious to know about the Rodgers, and they explained their situation to her, that they would be moving into town so that John could teach at Trinity.

"Where are you going to live?" she asked.

"Well, we'd like to be in the center of the village, close to the schools."

"When do you want to move?"

"Probably in June."

"How big a house will you need?"

"Big enough for our family of six."

"Well, my daughter owns a house, sort of where you want to be.

It's big enough, and the people are planning to move out soon. But my daughter is away now. She travels around to different colleges with a campus ministry. Would you like me to ask her about it the next time I see her?"

As the Rodgers nodded their interest, the daughter, who just happened to have come home unexpectedly the night before, walked into the kitchen! Of course, she was willing to show John and Blanche the house.

They saw it and knew it would be more than adequate for their needs. But they were sure it would be too expensive for the small school. They expressed to Bishop Stanway their willingness to live in a smaller place.

"Let me talk to her," he said.

A short time later, he came back grinning, "This has the mark of the hand of God on it!"

And he explained that they had agreed to mutually beneficial terms.

Of course, the house was more than adequate for their needs. And the way it came about was a great encouragement to John and Blanche. It was a clear illustration to them of God providing in the way that the Stanways had talked about. It helped them to make what John called "that first big spiritual step of moving out of a more protected life".

Peter Davids was an American scholar who had studied under Professor F.F. Bruce at the University of Manchester in England. For the last couple of years, he had been teaching at a Bible college in Germany.

Though not an Episcopalian, he was intrigued with the call to Trinity, and felt led to accept it, agreeing to be confirmed in the Episcopal Church in Europe. He would teach both Old and New Testament in the first year, until another professor could be found to teach Old Testament.

For Peter and his wife and two young daughters, the move was a big change. They were relocating from one continent to another, and joining what was to them a new denomination. But God graciously confirmed His will to them, so that they had peace in making the decision.

Like the Rodgers, they too needed to find an affordable home in Sewickley. As they prayed, God answered once again. A small house which was scheduled to be torn down was available to rent. Only three blocks from St. Stephen's, and the Stanways, and the Rodgers, the house was adequately suited to their needs. God's provision continued to amaze and encourage the growing TESM community.

Meanwhile, Les Fairfield had been looking into other Episcopal schools, but was not sensing that any of them was right for him.

He called the TESM office in the spring of 1976 and found that there were openings in the first class. He had not been able to get the support of his diocese in Indiana, so he had nothing to lose by coming to Trinity, and his home church in Lafayette was encouraging him to step out. So he applied to Trinity and was accepted as a student and, in a unique arrangement, was hired as a lecturer in Church History.

"It was scary to sign on with this new venture," recalled Les. "But at the same time, I had a sense that this was real, this was right. There was almost a boyish exuberance to Alf that would sneak out unexpectedly. It was infectious!"

And of course, God provided in a clear way for the Fairfields and their three small children. Lynn called realtors about homes for rent and received discouraging news. One agent said, "We haven't had rentals like that in several years!" A few minutes later she called back and said, "We just got a rental!"

In each instance, God was sovereignly drawing the people He had chosen. They had come from different backgrounds and different locations. But they united with great anticipation in this School which was being dramatically raised up by God to play a significant role in the renewing of the Church.

6
What Will the End Product Be?

Along with the Board members, Bishop Stanway prayed that God would send students who would be leaders, risk-takers who would be willing to attend Trinity even though it wasn't accredited. He really wasn't concerned with the quantity of students; he felt that the School could open its doors, even with a few, if they had a strong sense of call.

There was no Admissions Committee to review the earliest applicants for Trinity. There were very few procedures. And yet, acceptance was not automatic.

Bishop Stanway asked prospective students to write up an account of their personal relationship with Jesus Christ. He ascertained whether or not they had already demonstrated gifts for ministry and Christian leadership within a congregation or Christian organization. He stressed to candidates his intent that this school be rigorous academically in order to meet the Church's requirements. He interviewed married students along with their spouses, believing it crucial that both partners concur with the calling.

When the School opened, there were seventeen students in all. Though some had initiated contacts with their bishops, not one was being officially sent as a postulant from any diocese. Many came from the Pittsburgh area, or from southern states, but one also came from as far away as California, another from Massachusetts. Some were single, others were married and had children.

They had heard about Trinity in many different ways. Several students learned of the School through hearing Board members speak at their churches or universities. Most had "just happened" to pick up the news from someone who had heard someone else who was told by someone else...Virtually all had been affected by the renewal movement which had been growing in the early seventies. They had come to a personal faith in Christ, and were wrestling with a call to Biblically-based Christian ministry. It was with a sense of being pioneers that they moved to Sewickley to begin their studies.

September 25, 1976, dawned warm and sunny, a year to the day after Bishop Stanway had arrived in the United States. The brightness and clarity of the weather enhanced the happiness and expectancy surrounding the opening convocation. Two hundred and fifty people gathered in an auditorium at Robert Morris College to celebrate the occasion.

Peter Moore welcomed the guests and spoke about the contribution Trinity hoped to make to the life of the Episcopal Church. John Rodgers addressed the group about "Some Reasons for and Benefits of Theological Education for Ministry in the Anglican Evangelical Perspective". And Bishop Stanway spoke about the kind of graduate he hoped the school would produce.

"We want men and women of God. There are many things that we could say on an occasion like this; the scholarship that we hope to engender, the skills we hope to develop, the techniques we hope to impart—and they'll all be there. There will be no shortcuts in this seminary. The students have been warned by me when they were interviewed. It's a good, hard-working institution. They'll have to adapt themselves to that kind of a life, if they're going to be members of Trinity Episcopal School for Ministry. What governs any organization are the goals that they have set. And the goal we have is the kind of leader we want to train.

"I want to tell you what I think that kind of person ought to be. First of all, somebody who is unashamed of the gospel of Christ. Paul says he is unashamed of it because it is the power of God unto salvation for everyone that believes, unashamed of it because of its content, the content of the gospel that speaks of our glorious Lord and Savior, Jesus Christ. It raises Him up as the great name above all names in Heaven and on earth. It is the one real hope that will meet the needs of all mankind. Second, [he is unashamed] because of its truth—for if the gospel is not true, we have no message to proclaim, we have no right to be in the church of God at all. Thirdly, [the gospel has] power. God has the power to change lives. We want the students to know that power in their own lives, how greatly He can change their lives and set them free, and then to see it in the lives of others and in those to whom they minister "And certainly I want them to be men and women of prayer. It's not enough to be able to teach about prayer or to talk about prayer, but they must need to be able to go to the secret place and know that they will be heard. They go there so their ministries may be enriched after leaving this school; so that their sermons may be alive; so that their counseling may do what it's meant to do—to draw people back to God; and so that their pastoral care may be gracious and loving; and so that they themselves, because they have been men and women of prayer, will be free of anxiety, and therefore, able to be set free to do the work of the Lord.

"Then they should be liberated persons. That word has so many connotations, but I always speak of it in the Biblical sense. Jesus said, 'You shall know the truth, and the truth shall set you free.' 'If the Son shall set you free, you shall be free indeed'...The freedom that Christ gives, the real freedom from the bondage of sin, the freedom from those habits that keep a person from being the kind of leader God meant him to be. Then the freedom from the deadness of self-interest. You can feel the sadness in Paul's life when he is writing to the Philippian Church and says, 'I have no man whom I can send, for they all seek their own, not the things of Jesus Christ.' And then he spoke of Timothy. The whole thing changes. Shortly he can send Timothy—Timothy, the different one; Timothy, the one who first of all sought the things of Jesus Christ. The sad thing is that people can be in the ministry and not seek first the kingdom of God. We hope that those who go to this school will be delivered from the deadness of self-interest.

"Then, the students need to be set free of the love of money and possessions. Americans are very rich people indeed, and have a very large share of the world's goods. And some people feel that somehow or other, when you give up a great deal to become a minister of the gospel of Christ and serve the Lord, you won't have a temptation for the love of things or the love of money. Paul wrote to Timothy to beware of the love of money because some, having loved it, pierced themselves through with many sorrows. It doesn't matter whether you have a lot or whether you have a little—you can still be possessed by the love of money. And because you've been without, you may desire it more than some who've got it, and it's always a dead path for the minister of the gospel of Christ.

"A man was about to go to a parish recently and he came to consult me. 'What shall I say about my salary?' I said, 'Tell them to put it down in black and white what they are going to give you, set down the terms of service, and tell them in advance that you'll take what they give you.' He said, 'Do you mean that?' I said, 'I mean that absolutely. Take what they'll give you.' There are only two ways for the minister of the gospel of Christ. He can look after his own interests, and God will let him. Or he can look after the interests of the kingdom of God, and God will look after his interests. So I've found it.

"And then the students need to be delivered of the tyranny of the love of the world. John puts it very strongly when he says, 'If any man love the world, the love of the Father is not in him.' What is the love of the world? Well, some people break it down to definitions of little, small things. I like the definition that Archbishop Fisher gave when he visited us in East Africa. He said that the world is all that portion of society that is organized outside of three great principles: The sovereign rule of God, the redemption that is in Christ Jesus, and the life of the world to come. He went on to say that a great deal of society is organized outside those principles. That is society where this world is their horizon, where there is nothing up and over and beyond this world. But if the students are going to be delivered from those things, they're going to be bound by other things. They're going to be bound as the slaves of Christ. In the old slave laws, when a man was due to go out after his seven years, if he wanted to, he could go to his master and say, 'I love my master, I will not go out free.'

"If we love our Master, we will not go out free. We are committed and bound by that commitment to our Lord, Jesus Christ, bound by our baptismal promises, some of us bound by ordination, bound by the secret moment when we told the Lord we would give him all there is of our lives. And that commitment is there. But, accepting Christ as our Lord and Master is the very key to life itself. That's what integrates personality, that's what establishes purpose in life. I read the other day about Bertrand Russell. He said, 'Purpose? There is no purpose in life. It's like a leaf on a tree. It can go anywhere. The only purpose is the purpose of a fiend.' But the Christian has found his purpose in his commitment to his Lord and Master, Jesus Christ. He is also bound by his indebtedness to preach the gospel.

"Paul says, 'Woe is me if I preach not the gospel, I am a debtor both to the Jew and the Greek.' How can a person be a recipient of the grace of God and not want to take it to others? I want to say that if someone is unconcerned with the spread of the gospel of Christ, it must be a very weak kind of grace that he's got hold of. There is nothing plainer than this, that if a person really loves the Lord and depends on Him for the whole of his salvation, he wants to make that claim known to others. Then he is indebted to preach God's word and teach God's word...It's from the word of God that we get our instruction. It's not just that God has spoken long ago and that has been recorded in the word of God—it's not that God **has** spoken, but God speaks **today** through His word. There is a quotation, 'We have devised a method of studying the word of God out of which no word from God ever comes.' If God hasn't spoken, then we have no message to proclaim: if God has spoken, we have a message to preach. Woe be to us if we preach some other message.

"Then the fourth mark of the students we want is that they shall be seekers after holiness. I didn't know that word was so bad in the States. The writer to the Hebrews says, 'Holiness without which no man will see the Lord.' 'Be ye holy,' says the scripture,...'because I am holy.' It is the mark of Christian people. When a Christian and a minister of God gives up the battle for holiness, he's already a back-slider at heart. Whenever he reaches a stage where he is satisfied with his progress in the Christian life,....he is a back-slider. 'I've not yet attained,' [says Paul]. Always in the Christian life there is more beyond. And always the more we walk with God, the more we'll be discontented with the quality of life we have. For there are riches, better things beyond, and we should be marked by that desire for holiness. Paul, the Apostle, said, 'I make it my ambition to please Christ in all things.' One single sentence can change the life and pattern of a person. That is his aim, in his home life, in his study, in his work, in his witness, in his reading, in his giving, in his day by day conversations—in his ambition to please Christ.

"I remember when we were being trained for the compulsory military training we had in Australia (and it was done in spare time, too) we had to go down to the rifle range and qualify every year in shooting; and if you didn't qualify, you had to keep shooting until you did. The great thing was to qualify quickly. I remember the first time I went down there, there was a chap next to me who was waving his gun around and waving and waving. And the Sergeant-Major came and had one look at him, and he said, 'Man, if you aim at nothing, you're bound to hit it.' What are you aiming at? Are you like Paul, who said, 'I make it my ambition to please Christ in all things.'?

"Then a leader needs to have compassion for the poor and needy. And the most needy are those without the gospel of Christ. I was recently going to speak on evangelism at a diocesan conference, and the Diocesan Bishop wanted to know about the 'Bishop from Australia', so he rang me up to have a visit—to have what he called a visit with me on the telephone. He wanted to make quite sure I wasn't against social action. We talked for a little while about the first blind school in Tanganyika, which was in our diocese; the first leprosy work; the hospitals, the adult literacy campaigns; malnutrition; the first operations for corneal grafts to give sight to the blind. He was quite happy.

"But it is a mark of the Christian to have compassion. Jesus looked at that 'great crowd of people' and he had compassion upon them. The disciples said, 'Let us send them away.' And Jesus said, 'There is no need to send them away. Give ye them to eat.'

"Then they should be people who are alive with the life of the Spirit of God. What's the good in being able to speak well, to be sound in doctrine, and know the way you ought to live if the whole of your life is not made alive with the Spirit of God? There is one mark which the Spirit of God can give to people who are called ministers that will make people know that they are God's leaders, and it is this: when they speak, men and women will hear God's voice speaking through them. Then they'll know. That's our 'imprimatur'. It's greater than any degree you can get from Trinity School. It's greater than any qualifications you can get in the United States or elsewhere. It's better than any praise that men can give you. That imprimatur of the Spirit of God himself—if you speak, then people hear God speaking to them. Then they know you are a person of God.

"Then finally, the students need to be gripped with a deep sense of gratitude for the privilege of being called to be Christ's servant. For if ever a leader begins to think what he is putting into the ministry, or what great favor he is performing for the people that he is ministering to or the organization which he has joined, he's half dead. There is nothing quite like the privilege of being God's servant. I want to put this kind of question to all of you today: if other people knew you like God knows you, all your faults and all your thoughts, all your sins, all the things in your heart that have ever been there, all the wrong thoughts that you've ever had, would they trust you with the kind of work that God trusts you with? Here is the supreme confidence that God has in His own grace. He'll take the likes of you and me and give us the privilege of being His servant. He's got to take people like you and me—He has no others. That's the only kind that He possesses. People who are at best weak men, weak women, made strong. The Christian life is not a case of girding up your loins and saying, 'I will be strong.' It is a case of acknowledging your weakness. Paul said, 'When I am weak, then I am strong, for God's strength is made perfect in weakness.' When a leader loses the sense of gratitude for being called to God's service, then there is something very wrong with his work in ministry.

"To this end, we dedicate ourselves. Our hope is that from this class every single one will go out and be effective in God's service. And my dream is that from this first batch of students, there will come such a development of God's Spirit on some of them that they will be those who will go out and make Christ's name known and ring across the United States of America...May God who has called us to His service, make us faithful in our calling."

7

The Formation of Spiritual Leaders

Trinity's founders were deliberate in their choice of a name for the school.

The word "Trinity" emphasized their belief in and worship of all three persons of the Godhead, Father, Son, and Holy Spirit.

"Episcopal" indicated their commitment to the denomination. They had been deeply touched by the various renewal movements springing up in the Church, and desired to strengthen that renewal so that the Episcopal Church could fulfill its task of increasing the glory of God by making the Name of Jesus Christ known.

And "School for Ministry" proclaimed that this new institution was concerned with the ministry of the whole Body of Christ. In addition to the usual three-year M.Div. program, it offered a one-year course designed to train lay people to faithfully exercise their gifts in ministry. And it aimed to strike a balance between academic and practical training for the students preparing for the ordained ministry, with the intent that these future clergy see one of their primary tasks as that of equipping the saints for ministry.

One of the first things the new students became aware of was the academic excellence being offered to them, and required of them. Bishop Stanway was a disciplined man, and expected the School to be a hard-working institution. Board members were adamant that standards be set high in order that graduates be fully qualified for effective ministry, and able to establish a solid reputation for the School. From the beginning, the faculty members submitted their students to outside testing to be certain that Trinity's training was at least commensurate with what was offered in other seminaries.

Gospel Presuppositions For Gospel Ends

The demanding curriculum reflected the School's "deep confidence in the Holy Scriptures as the Word of God written", and the belief that "God's people must be deeply shaped by the Bible". John Rodgers explained this perspective of Anglican Evangelicalism in his address at the opening convocation:

"God's Word in Christ has been lost and obscured by the manner in which we approach God's Word written. Legitimate critical scholarship has increasingly married itself to false assumptions and presuppositions, and the church is left with a Bible which has been reduced to the more or less interesting speculations and curious thoughts of men and women of an earlier age. When the authority, sufficiency, clarity, and efficacy of the Holy Scriptures are lost, then we are left with human speculation, tentative gropings, and finally—*silence*........

"We hope at Trinity so to search the Scriptures together that from this time of study will come persons into the life of the Church who can share this confidence; humbly, lovingly, intelligently, and persuasively. At this point we have a great contribution to make, and there can be little doubt that the Church needs most profoundly this contribution of confidence in and wise, sane interpretation of the Holy Scriptures as the Word of God written..."

And so, a full thirty-five percent of the course work focused on the study of the Old and New Testaments, and the content of the remaining courses was centered on and shaped by Scriptural truth. Faculty members combined their knowledge of their field with their personal love of the Lord Jesus Christ to make sometimes "dry" subjects come to life.

One alumnus remembers his first year of systematic theology as being a powerful time in his own growth and formation. He grew so much in his understanding of who God is and of how He has worked in the affairs of humanity that he found class to be a worshipful experience, often leaving him feeling as though he were "filled with helium".

Another commented that during his first year he chafed under the academic emphasis, wishing he could be "doing ministry" more practically. As he looks back, though, he is profoundly grateful for the Scriptural foundation he received, saying, "At Trinity, I was given a lot of information, but more importantly, I picked up a lot of tools for feeding myself and others from the Scriptures. I've had plenty of time to learn the practical things since I graduated. I have the rest of my life to spend helping hurting people."

Personal Spirituality

Similarly, there has been, from the beginning, an emphasis on the need for individual students to develop personal spiritual disciplines in the context of a relationship with the living Lord Jesus Christ. The required chapel service started late enough to give students time for a period of prayer at home before the start of the day. The cultivation of such a close walk with God was essential to a "ministry" full of both content and power.

Bishop Stanway provided strong leadership in this area. Prayer, and trust in a loving heavenly Father, were the very fabric of his spiritual life. Challenging students to be disciplined to keep a daily quiet time of prayer and personal Bible Study, he once commented that, with God's help, he had not missed a quiet time in forty years. When asked what one thing had helped him the most in his ministry, he responded without missing a beat, "Getting up at 6 a.m. with a pot of tea and my Bible."

In his class on prayer, he would say, "The prayer you should pray most in your life is this: 'Teach us to pray'. If you think you've learned, then you'll never be a person of prayer. There's always more to learn, more to discover about prayer."

He taught that Nehemiah was a great leader because he combined prayer with action. His hard work, his choice of good leaders, the courage of his convictions, his self-control, all of these were possible only because he listened to God's voice. The same principle applied to those who were preparing for ministry.

Field Training

Bishop Stanway and the Board insisted that practical ministry training be at the heart of the curriculum. Trinity was to be a vocational school, not just a university. While academic study was important, it would be useless if it resulted in insulating students from the world to which they were being trained to minister. As faith without works is dead, so the academic learning without actual ministry experience would be counterproductive.

The first year, field education was somewhat inchoate. A number of students participated in ministry programs at St. Stephen's Church in Sewickley, but without much supervision or actual training. In the second year, the Rev. Mike Henning was called from his position as Youth Minister at St. Stephen's to teach practical theology at TESM and to organize a field education program.

Mike's goal was to link students with mentors in a "strength on strength" placement. Seminarians were not just to be a cheap source of labor with which parishes could fill in the holes in their ministries. Instead, field education supervisors were considered adjunct faculty. They were asked to identify their own strengths, and then were paired with students with similar strengths. In a sacrificial way, they were to allow students to come alongside them to learn ministry by doing it in their stead, with their guidance.

It was a plan with a lofty ideal, and in many instances it worked. Bishop Appleyard of the Diocese of Pittsburgh encouraged parishes to accept seminarians for field training, saying that the individual churches had much to offer to Trinity students. So, many churches, some of which did not agree with the theological perspective of Trinity, nonetheless took on students for field education.

In the first few years, though nearly twenty-five parishes were involved in the field education program, there was an overwhelmingly positive response to the ministry of Trinity people. Significant ministry was occurring in the local parishes. Students started Bible studies. They worked closely with teenagers. They preached Biblically-based sermons. Some were involved with one-on-one pastoral care. In some instances, churches either immediately or eventually called their seminarian or another Trinity graduate to a full-time ministry position!

And as requests continued to come in for Trinity faculty to lead renewal weekends in parishes around the country, more and more students went along on those trips. They grew in their ministry skills and experience, but they were especially invigorated as they looked forward to the days when they would be doing full-time what they were now training to do.

Missions

The presence of Bishop Stanway made mission a central part of Trinity's life and identity. There was an emphasis on training students for mission work at home and abroad, and on equipping students from other cultures for leadership in their native countries.

Many people think only of "missions" in monetary terms. The word is a line item in a church budget. Or it's associated with mite boxes and other forms of raising money. It's something most people "give to" instead of "go on".

But Christian mission is something entirely different. It means going wherever God sends you, to work in His Name, bringing the message of hope and reconciliation, healing, teaching, helping in the Name of Jesus Christ. It is a "given" with Trinity's theological perspective because being a grateful recipient of the "good news" necessarily implies sharing it, whether you travel five miles across town to do so, or five thousand miles around the world.

Through Bishop Stanway, the Trinity community became aware of the great revival that had been sweeping East Africa for decades. They grieved together at the murder of his friend, Archbishop Janani Luwum of Uganda, who was killed in early 1977, probably by Idi Amin himself. They were moved by the work and witness of Bishop Festo Kivengere of Uganda, who, having barely escaped from his country with his life, was one of TESM's first guest speakers.

In the second year, a Kenyan priest, Charles Gaikia Gaita, came to study at Trinity. And ever since then, a steady stream of students from foreign countries has come to Ambridge to be trained for Christian leadership. Their presence has enriched the life of the community, increasing awareness of the hand of God at work in different parts of the world, and kindling in many a sense of call to serve Him in faraway places.

In 1983, Geoff Little, a Lay Studies student training for missionary work with the South American Missionary Society, acted as a catalyst for the development of a Missions Committee. This student-led group met weekly to pray for specific missionaries and for unreached people groups. The participants sought to raise the awareness of overseas missions among the Trinity community. They made special banners and established an annual "Missions Day". Through their efforts, some students sensed God calling them to such missionary work.

In the first fifteen years, 53 of Trinity's graduates served as ambassadors of the gospel in 24 different countries. And those who remained in the United States brought to their congregations a heightened awareness of and support for those who were working for Christ in other cultures.

A Worshipping Community

Another goal of Trinity's founders was the development of an authentic, caring, worshipping Christian community. One of the first guest speakers in the fall of 1976, the Rev. Michael Green, then from St. Aldate's Church, Oxford, in England, stressed the need to spend time building good interpersonal relationships.

In the first few years of Trinity's life, this close fellowship seemed to happen without much orchestration. There was a strong unity of purpose and sense of pioneering that drew people together. Faculty members and their wives met together regularly for prayer and fellowship. Most faculty and students lived within walking distance of each other in the town of Sewickley. The whole community gathered on Thursdays for a soup dinner, and service of the Lord's Supper.

Each school day began with a half-hour worship service in the classroom. The leader and preacher were both students. The form varied between liturgical and non-liturgical. Bishop Stanway was convinced that both kinds could be alive with the power of God.

After a few years, advisee groups were developed which gave students a place to share concerns and to develop some accountability. A support group grew up for spouses. Attempts to gather the increasing number of people together became more deliberate.

For most, this degree of sharing met needs for fellowship. But, as one faculty wife commented, about six weeks into the fall semester of every year, there would inevitably be a student sermon on the importance of transparency in relationships. Whether singles or couples, those who desired to be more closely linked with others usually found each other and formed deeper fellowships within the larger community.

Most graduates look back on their time at TESM with gratitude and are overwhelmingly positive in commending the School. They give to it financially, and urge their parishes to do so. They encourage prospective students to attend. They return for reunions and continuing education courses. The spiritual formation they received at Trinity was a watershed in their own discipleship as Christians and in their role of equipping God's people to do His work.

8
Growing Pains

E veryone knew that Trinity's location on the campus of Robert Morris College was only temporary. Bishop Stanway had challenged the Board back in January of 1976, months before the School had opened, that it would need to press on in praying and working toward a permanent location.

In the middle of the Board members' euphoria over their unanimous decision to move ahead with arrangements at Robert Morris, the Bishop asked them to pray and think ahead about buying land. He encouraged them to seek God's face humbly, as they had been learning to do all along. He reminded them of the need to be concerned with pleasing Him, of committing their hearts and minds to doing whatever He showed to be His will.

A year later, in January of 1977, the Board, still praying, did not yet know God's mind about a permanent site, but there was a general feeling that such a location was needed soon. As they prayed and waited, facts began to come together to support that feeling.

By May, the end of the first year of school, John Rodgers reported to the Board that he and the rest of the faculty hoped to be at Robert Morris only one more year. The initial classroom and office space, though adequate at the time, was cramped, and the problem would only get worse with another class of students coming in.

The winter had been severe; the bridge over the Ohio River between Robert Morris and Sewickley, where most faculty and married students lived, had been closed. It was increasingly difficult to get the whole community together.

In addition, the cold weather had caused Robert Morris to shut down for several weeks. Trinity had remained open by holding classes at St. Stephen's Church in Sewickley. As the School grew larger, it would no longer have that flexibility, but would be more dependent on the decisions made by its landlord. With its own facility, TESM could set its own schedule.

To be sure, a permanent location would cost a lot of money. But on the other hand, more people would probably give to the School once it was clearly settled for the long term. They would be more willing to donate funds to an endowment campaign for degree-granting status if the school owned its own buildings. Anyway, God had already demonstrated that He was fully able to provide whatever was needed.

Many circumstances seemed to confirm the leading that Pittsburgh would be a good location. The Lord had already given strong guidance that He was leading TESM to Pittsburgh by the providential way in which housing had been found for so many faculty and student families. The Diocese of Pittsburgh had proven to be open to the presence of Trinity students in parishes for field education. There was an increasing number of clergy and laity in the Diocese who were open to the renewal movement. The Bishop was friendly to Trinity. There was no other Episcopal seminary nearby. There was a growing number of financially committed people.

It was time to look into the available options, and there were many.

George Oliver, Treasurer of TESM since 1976, remembers that Bishop Stanway insisted on being open to any possibility that the Lord might send to them. As a number of suggested locations came up, he was determined to pursue each one in order to discover which way God was leading.

One piece of property was a large parcel of undeveloped land up in the hills near Sewickley. George felt it would be pointless to waste time looking at it, but the Bishop was adamant about seeing everything

Another time, George learned of a set of apartments that were for sale. Some of the buildings could be gutted and redesigned, but the project would require a large investment of time and money. Again, Bishop Stanway wanted to see the property. He wanted a specific indication from the Lord as to whether this were the place He was providing.

"I think we should pray about it and take a look at it."

So he and George bowed their heads and prayed briefly about it. When they said "Amen", George lifted his head, and saw that the Bishop, not one to waste time, was already up and out the door!

They drove to the apartments, parked, and walked in one of the access roads, only to find the owner and another man coming down the sidewalk toward them. George went over and introduced Bishop Stanway to the owner, who in turn introduced the man with him, saying, "I'd like you to meet the new owner."

They exchanged a few pleasantries and then, as the Bishop and George walked back to the car, the Bishop commented in his terse way, "A clear indication!"

George reflected that he was impressed by Bishop Stanway's attitude. "My reaction would have been to kick myself for not looking into the property sooner. But he wasn't bothered by a closed door. He just went on to look at the other possibilities."

Marjory Stanway concurred, "Alf never went to bed concerned about that kind of thing. He was prepared to accept each proposed location as it came up, if that was right. But when a door closed, he didn't worry. He always felt that God would show us what was right. As each thing proved fruitless, he'd say, 'Well, God must have something better.'"

A piece of property which seemed promising was located across the river. Set off away from the businesses and the airport, it would have been ideal for a campus. It was a pastoral setting conducive to study and reflection. But there were a few complications with the title, and it fell through. And as they reflected on why it wasn't right, the people involved began to feel that God was calling them to be in the midst of a community, not isolated in a near-monastic setting.

So they looked closely at an old elementary school property in the heart of Sewickley. It seemed ideal, across the street from St.

Stephen's Church, within blocks of the homes of faculty and married students. But opposition began to mount from the community of Sewickley itself. Ostensibly, the reason was a loss of property from the tax rolls. Some residents bluntly said, "We don't want a lot of noisy seminarians."

At first, the TESM community wondered if this were the normal kind of digging in of heels that occurs in the world or among non-Christian people when God's will is being done. Was this the type of opposition that could be prayed away? Parted like the Red Sea? Walked around like the walls of Jericho? Were they to press on, or take "no" for an answer?

At one point, John Rodgers told Bishop Stanway, "I haven't given up that piece of land yet!"

And the Bishop responded that he hadn't either. "I don't know whether we're meant to have it or not meant to have it. I can't tell, but what I know is this. If we were to get it now, we'd know that God gave it to us. And if we get something better, we'll know that God gave us that, too. If God closes a door, no man can open it. If God opens a door, no man can shut it."

With the passage of time, it became clear that the borough of Sewickley would not budge. Some students and faculty were distressed, but the Bishop seemed unconcerned. He said, "We don't want to settle where we're not wanted."

After months of fruitless searching, John and Blanche Rodgers happened to attend a dinner sponsored by a local civic group. John hadn't even felt up to going—he had come home tired and cold, and wanted to spend the evening at home. But Blanche had already bought tickets, so that was that!

They ended up sitting near a lawyer and his wife who, though they lived in Sewickley, attended a Presbyterian Church in Ambridge, a steel town six miles to the north. As they chatted, John spoke of Trinity and of the challenge of trying to find a permanent location. And the lawyer described his work, including his service on the board of a nearby Christian college. The four of them enjoyed the fellowship of meeting new friends and discovering that they all knew and loved God and were committed to serving Him.

About a month later, the lawyer telephoned John with the news that his church had decided to merge with another Presbyterian church in Ambridge, and would be selling its old building. The congregation hoped that the building would continue to be used for Christian work. Would Trinity be interested in buying it?

George Oliver, John Rodgers, and Bishop Stanway went up to Ambridge to look at the church. It was perfect, ready-made for the School's current needs. There were several large classrooms; some smaller rooms could be used for offices; there was a commons room down by the kitchen. George even noted the nave-type of construction, unusual for a Presbyterian Church, but well-suited to an Anglican style of worship.

There was just one problem. The church was on a small lot right on the main street through town.

"What about parking?" they asked the man who was showing them around.

"Oh, see that A&P across the street? They let us use their lot."

"Well, that's fine for Sunday. But a school will need a parking lot every day of the week."

"Didn't you know? The A&P is for sale also!"

And then, as though a light bulb had clicked on inside his head, John Rodgers remembered something the librarian at Virginia Theological Seminary had once said to him. He had warned John that old mansions were not good buildings to convert into libraries. They were not constructed to hold the weight of so many books. A storefront with a large flat surface would be much more conducive to being used as a library.

And here it was!

Both pieces of property, close together, for sale at the same time...

But even more amazing was the fact that the combined price was almost exactly equal to the amount that Mrs. Chalfant had given three years earlier!

The Chairman of the Board, Peter Moore, flew to Pittsburgh and toured the facilities with George, John, and the Bishop. The question now before them was, "Does the School wish to locate in a place such as Ambridge?"

Just as the English reformers a few centuries earlier had met at the White Horse Inn to discuss the issues before them, these four wandered a block and a half down the street from the Presbyterian Church to Mad Anthony's Restaurant where they could sit down, and share their concerns. And as they talked and prayed, they decided to encourage the Board to give permission to buy the two buildings.

Two students with experience in construction led a work crew of students in renovating the Presbyterian church building over the summer of 1978. They quickly did a thorough job, keeping costs low (another example of God's provision), and the building was ready when school opened again in September, with a chapel, classrooms, and a common room. The "library" consisted of books stored on rolling carts, or on makeshift shelves of planks and cement blocks!

Over the next winter, the School borrowed money, which was quickly repaid with extra donations, to begin remodeling the A & P, which would hold the library, offices for faculty and administrative staff, the bookstore, and some storage space. The new building was ready in time for the following school year 1979-80.

Steve Noll, who had recently arrived to join the faculty, recalls "the procession of the books from the chapel building, carried on shelves by students like the ark of the covenant, across the street, and laid down on rectangles marked on the carpet with chalk— two thousand volumes alphabetically by author"!

Bishop Appleyard came to lead a service of dedication and expressed thankfulness for the ministry of seminarians doing field work in local parishes, and for the leadership of John Rodgers. It was an exhilarating time of deep gratitude for the visible evidence of all that God had brought about in four short years.

In hindsight, some of God's purpose for the School in providing the Ambridge property has become clear. Those who come to Trinity have had to give up the affluent American Dream. They spend three or more years in a mill town that has seen better days. Even when the School purchased the property, Ambridge had declined from the post-World War II boom of the steel industry.

Several years later, the slowdown of the early 1980's hit the town hard. Plants closed. Many workers found themselves without a job. A substantial number of families moved away in an attempt to get work elsewhere.

Ambridge is also made up of people from a variety of ethnic heritages. Many of these individuals are the children and grandchildren of immigrants who settled there specifically to work in the steel mills. These pockets of ethnicity have remained distinct, and have provided a rich and diverse background for the town. And yet, the setting bears no resemblance to the generally assumed "Anglican ethos" of intellectualism, prestige, power, and wealth.

It is this very ordinary quality of the town that has been an asset to students training for ministry, for more reasons than just that the cost of living is relatively low. Jesus warned repeatedly of the dangers of greed, which will destroy the soul of the Christian. And in our sales-oriented society, it's difficult to keep from being preoccupied with material things. As John Rodgers commented wryly from his office in the former meat section of the supermarket, "Nobody comes here because of the beauty of the buildings or the campus!"

At the same time, graduates have not been ill-equipped to serve wealthy parishes. Rather, they have had occasion to learn to put first God's kingdom and His righteousness, and have seen firsthand His faithfulness in meeting needs. They are generally prepared to lead Christians anywhere in a Biblical view of stewardship which receives gratefully from God all that He has supplied, and gives back generously for the sake of the spread of the gospel.

Similarly, the identity of the School has been shaped by God's "No" to Sewickley. Although John Guest's leadership was crucial in the early years, it was not to be his seminary or a St. Stephen's training center. By the same token, it was not to be Bishop Stanway's, or Peter Moore's, or John Rodgers' school either.

Instead, in a location of its own, Trinity is a school for the whole Episcopal Church, offering itself and its graduates as instruments of renewal and reformation.

9

The Mantle Passes

Bishop Stanway felt that one of the marks of a good leader was the ability to devolve, to cause the leadership of a ministry to pass easily into the hands of a successor. So he had initially planned to stay in the United States four years, heading back to Australia after the first class graduated in June of 1979.

By October of 1977, he was beginning to feel that he didn't have quite the same energy he had had two years earlier. He thought that God might be telling him not to renew his work permit for a fourth year.

The Board had known that it would have to choose another Dean/President to succeed him sooner or later. Now Bishop Stanway urged the members to look closely at the matter.

It was generally felt that the new Dean did not necessarily have to have a Ph.D. but it was crucial that he hold firm the spiritual standards of the school, and keep the staff, faculty, and students working closely in harmony.

The logical choice seemed to be John Rodgers. He had been with the school from the beginning. He was a gifted scholar. He had developed great rapport with the students. He had developed confidence in God and as a leader. Bishop Stanway respected his wisdom, his gentleness, and his knowledge of the American Church.

In November, the Bishop traveled to Tanzania for the celebration of the golden anniversary of the diocese of which he had been bishop for twenty years. While he was there, he visited with one of his friends, a doctor who had not seen him for six or seven years. This man was startled to see that the Bishop's face had become like a mask, much less expressive than he remembered. He suspected Parkinson's disease, and insisted that Bishop Stanway be tested. The diagnosis was confirmed before he returned to the United States.

He began taking strong L-dopa medications. While he was mentally alert, he felt somewhat strange. His energy was flagging, and he spoke of a "loss of liberty in speech and expression", though he didn't have tremors or problems with walking. His primary concern was that he didn't want to be a drag on the School. In the spring, he submitted his resignation, effective October 31, 1978.

The Board members were distressed at the thought of the Stanways leaving so soon. But they also knew that it would be better for them to face a progressive disease in their own country, among their many Christian friends, and with the support they would receive from Australia's national health care system.

So, the Board quickly stepped up its search. It felt it was important for the new Dean to work with the Bishop for a short while, not just to learn the ways of the school, but also to benefit from his spiritual leadership. While John Rodgers seemed a natural choice, it was essential to consider other qualified candidates, though there were few of them.

Bishop Stanway continued to speak highly of John. He felt he had an exceptional academic and theological ability, saying of him, "Cut him anywhere, and theology pours out". John had formed positive relationships with the students and the staff, and was able to put visitors at ease. He had the gift of expressing great truths simply. He was eager to move toward accreditation and to build up the library. The Bishop would not hesitate to select him.

By May of 1978, it was time for a vote. The Bishop addressed the concerns of a few in regard to John's administrative ability. "He has handled everything well...You will not find his equivalent in many years' search; he is good all round."

So John was unanimously elected Dean/President, effective November 1, 1978.

The installation date was set for October 15, at the close of a national PEWSaction Renewal Conference, which was to be held in Pittsburgh. The conference, similar to the one four years earlier in Atlanta where John Guest had made the startling announcement of a new school, and to the one in New York the following year at the time of the first Board meeting, gathered more than thirteen hundred people from across the country who were interested and active in renewal.

The School held workshops for people who wanted to learn more about Trinity. Many had never heard of the School before, and were thrilled to find out about it, and to participate in the worship service. Word about Trinity spread far more effectively than it would have through letters alone.

October fifteenth was a day of glorious celebration. The installation service was held in Trinity Cathedral in downtown Pittsburgh. That alone was cause for rejoicing. Robert Appleyard, Bishop of Pittsburgh, had been more receptive to the existence of Trinity Episcopal School for Ministry than had almost all other bishops, but he had still practiced a deliberate detachment, giving the School time to prove itself. Now, it was another expression of encouragement and support to the School that he invited the installation to be held in the Cathedral, and that he himself participated. And when he stepped forward to embrace John Rodgers during the passing of the Peace, the whole student body stood up and cheered!

A few months later, Bishop Appleyard made his first official visit to Trinity, celebrating a service of Holy Communion. In his remarks, he commended the School for the ministries its faculty and students had carried out in the Diocese of Pittsburgh.

He also gave the School two small glass cruets. These had been smuggled out of China by Bishop Huang over the Burma Road as he and other Chinese Christians fled the takeover of their country. He had given them to Bishop Appleyard, who in turn gave them to the School as a symbol of Trinity's outreach to the entire world.

And while Trinity was seeking to please God alone, of all the human affirmations that could have been given, this was the most precious. To the Trinity community, it was another tangible evidence of God's hand at work, another occasion of deep gratitude for all that He had done, another encouragement to press on with the mission God had given.

Even in the midst of the exhilaration over John Rodgers' installation, there was a desire to hold on to the moment, and postpone the approaching date of the Stanways' departure. On the day they left, the whole Trinity community gathered in a circle in front of the Olivers' home. It was the kind of Indian summer day that is captured in postcards—an early chill dissipating as the sun climbed higher—golden leaves gently letting go of their branches and wafting dutifully to the ground in the stillness—the ache in individual hearts intensified by the stabbing sunshine and the hint of frost.

Faculty, students, spouses, and children gathered around briefly to pray. The Stanways reassured them that they would hold each one up regularly in prayer. Then everyone shook hands, the Stanways settled into the car, and they were gone!

Peter Moore articulated his own sense of feeling bereft: "When Alf left, I was aghast. I said, 'How can he expect to leave a seminary to go on its own after three years?' I kept thinking, 'Can't we persuade him to stay longer?' And I did my best to do so, but he was adamant about it. So he must have known that we little chicks were ready to be pushed out of the nest, and learn to fly on our own, because he went away with utter confidence. He and Marjory packed their bags, and moved out of the house, and flew back to Australia, and left the rest of us here. And all of us had come to see him as a father in God, and somebody we would go to with our problems. And suddenly we were left on our own. And it was a scary moment.

"I was Chairman of the Board then. And it was then that I learned that I could lean rather heavily on John Rodgers, who took over the reins, and who became our Dean, and who brought to the school great vigor and vision. John knew the Church, and the Church knew John, and it made a tremendous difference to have him there. I feel that God was very gracious to give us a home-grown American for our second Dean, after having started with an Australian. John, it seemed to me, had the gift of faith, as Alf Stanway had."

10
Passing the Test

The approval of other people is a funny thing. Christians, seeking to play to an audience of One, shouldn't seek it or be motivated by it. But sometimes they need it, especially when they're running a Christian institution. Trinity needed to have degree-granting status with the Commonwealth of Pennsylvania, and accreditation with the Association of Theological Schools. Not many students would come if they weren't certain they would graduate with a bona fide degree. And bishops weren't likely to send their postulants and candidates to a brand-new school where the quality of the education had not been proven over time, or hadn't received some sort of official recognition.

So Trinity approached the accreditation process cautiously, wanting, on the one hand, to win official approval of the state and of the Association of Theological Schools in order to be accepted in the Episcopal Church. On the other, the School desired to please God in all things, and was determined not to compromise its identity and mission.

So all through the Board minutes, there is concern about meeting the necessary requirements. But at the same time, the voices of Bishop Stanway and John Rodgers come through, urging people to be patient, and to keep their eyes on God.

As the second year of classes began, the Board expressed a need for outside examinations, objective testing, to make sure TESM's classes were rigorous enough academically. Other theological schools gave evidence of widespread inflation of grades and therefore a loss of accountability. Many seminaries were not covering the basics. The results of the General Ordination Examinations taken by graduating seniors in some other schools that year were poor, indicating low standards. Even before beginning the process of accreditation, Trinity wanted to preclude the development of bad academic habits.

As the first students reached their senior year, some of them prepared to take the GOE's in January of 1979. These produced positive results. All five students who took the exams did well overall, especially on the objective part.

Over the next few years, it was clear that good performance on the GOE's was encouraging open but tentative bishops to ordain Trinity graduates. So the School continued to work students hard in order to prepare them for those exams.

Dr. Warren Evans, of the Pennsylvania Department of Education, visited Trinity along with a team of other educators in January of 1978 to make a preliminary evaluation of the School. Though Pennsylvania has some of the highest standards in the country, these men were impressed by what had been accomplished in less than three years, and urged the School to continue to develop on its current course.

Les Fairfield organized the preparation of a detailed report requiring documentation of finances, a long-range planning program, a description of the School's purpose and history, and explanations of policies covering every aspect of the School's life.

The only remaining hurdles were sufficient development of the library and the accumulation of a $500,000 endowment. John Rodgers challenged the Board to keep praying, and to move on ahead, trusting that God would provide the funds.

The School stepped up its search for books, and hired a full-time librarian. Soon the acquisition of volumes was outstripping the capacity of the staff to catalogue them. Then, in the fall of 1979, with more than twelve thousand volumes on hand, it just so happened that a local person was found who knew how to catalogue books according to the Library of Congress system. It was an amazing provision of someone who was to be living only temporarily in the Ambridge area.

Meanwhile, new Board member Martin Clark led the way in praying and working towards raising the money needed for the endowment, even as funds were also needed for scholarships, operating expenses, and renovations to the chapel and the supermarket. Continuing Bishop Stanway's pattern, he urged that they all trust God, minister sensitively, and make the School's needs known. Small gifts had already been earmarked for the endowment fund, and the value of contributed services could be applied to that total, but the need was still more than $400,000.

Over the next two years, as the whole Trinity community prayed, funds came in in a variety of ways—through individual gifts, parish gifts, appreciating stock, matching gift offers. Students who had not been at Trinity during the Robert Morris days were learning firsthand about the rich variety of God's provision.

Even as the school sought larger grants, it continued to operate under the "money follows ministry" principle. Members of foundations were invited to Trinity, to see how God had worked, to participate in the life of the community, and to catch the vision for the School's impact on the Church and the world.

And gifts followed. During the school year 1980-81, more than $750,000 was given to Trinity, a sharp escalation provided by the Lord to meet several large simultaneous needs!

Warren Evans and the rest of the evaluation team from the state made their final visit in February of 1981, and submitted a report in April to the Pennsylvania Secretary of Education, recommending that Trinity be given degree-granting status retroactively to the first class. Still, when Bishop and Mrs. Stanway made plans to travel to Pennsylvania in May, hoping to distribute degrees to all students from the first three years, there was no certainty that degree-granting status would be given and, if it were, that it would be retroactive.

In the middle of May, two weeks before graduation, Les Fairfield received the good news from Warren Evans. Hanging up the phone, he immediately called Bishop Stanway. The Bishop gave a terse response, but when he hung up and went to tell George Oliver, there were tears in his eyes.

From the beginning, Trinity was careful to keep bishops informed as to its vision and progress. The School sent out to all thirteen thousand Episcopal clergy a copy of *Kerygma*, the publication of the Fellowship of Witness, which reported Trinity's opening. Periodically, letters were sent to all bishops, apprising them of the School's status in the accreditation process.

Support among the bishops gradually increased. Though not a single bishop sent a student to the School in the first year, by the beginning of the second year, five bishops were sending students. A year later, the number had doubled to ten.

Bishops themselves were beginning to visit Trinity, and were very positive. One commented that there was a lively and refreshing sense of "calling" at this School which contrasted with a dryer "professionalism" elsewhere. Students at Trinity articulated an understanding that a personal God, the Father of the Lord Jesus Christ, had led them to train for the ordained ministry, sometimes giving up successful careers.

When the degree-granting status was approved, John Rodgers wrote to all the bishops again, telling them also of the consistently high GOE performance of TESM students, and of the progress being made toward accreditation with the Association of Theological Schools.

Even so, there was misunderstanding. Some bishops still thought that Trinity had started because John Rodgers and Fitz Allison, a founding Board member of TESM and Church History professor at Virginia Theological Seminary, had had a "snit" with VTS.

In some cases, there was unabashed opposition. One bishop responded to John's letter, "I was against TESM, and still feel it is a great mistake. I would not send any of my postulants."

But most responses expressed congratulations. Some pledged prayer support. Others wanted more information about the School.

When Presiding Bishop Allin spoke at Trinity's graduation in 1983, he praised the School for its "'dedication and perseverance which comes from faithfulness' and the humility and faith with which Trinity has nourished and encouraged the Church". He expressed confidence that the School would continue to have a positive impact on the Episcopal Church, especially through the ministry of its graduates.

Meanwhile, the Trinity Board and faculty were pressing on toward the most important milestone, accreditation with the the Association of Theological Schools.

ATS requirements were more stringent. Evaluators examined Trinity's statement of faith to ascertain that the School's policies and procedures were consistent with its own foundational documents.

They looked closely at the library, and required thirty to forty thousand catalogued volumes. This challenge was the most time-consuming and costly one for Trinity. At the rate at which the School was adding volumes in 1981, it would take nine years to reach the ATS accrediting level. Clearly, the process needed to speed up. Time seemed to be the problem more than money.

Again, John Rodgers advised the Board and the rest of the Trinity community to pray, to carry on, and not to panic.

Then in 1982, Seabury-Western and Garrett seminaries combined their library collections, leaving them with seventeen thousand excess volumes. Trinity made a bid for these, and was able to use two thirds of the collection; the providential timing of the purchase and the substantial number of already catalogued books put the School well on the way towards its goal.

The other major ATS requirement was a self-study detailing every facet of the School's life, and drawing on the views of faculty, staff, students, and alumni. Academic Dean Steve Noll headed up a committee which sent out numerous questionnaires and spent many hours tabulating the responses.

It was an arduous process, but the School was given a tentative approval when the ATS team made its final visit in March of 1985. When its Commission on Accreditation met in June, it finalized its acceptance, and Trinity Episcopal School for Ministry became the eleventh and newest accredited seminary in the Episcopal Church.

With accreditation, Trinity was now in a position to receive more donations from parishes. At the same time, the School would not abandon its policy of trusting the Lord to move people and parishes to give.

It was also hoped that accreditation would lead to an increase in Trinity's enrollment. Many bishops had not sent postulants to Trinity, citing the fact that it was not yet accredited. Though more and more had been doing so, the School anticipated an upturn in applications.

Trinity did, in fact, continue to receive more money from parishes and an increase in the total student enrollment, but there was no sharp increase during the next few years. Rather, the School continued to grow in a gradual upward curve of acceptance. A few more bishops responded favorably.

In 1988, the newly installed Presiding Bishop Edmund Browning visited Trinity at the invitation of the Board. Later, he commented, "I was very grateful to have been asked to come. You get all sorts of impressions about places from their reputation. I try to go with an open spirit about everything, and I was very moved by the work that Dean Rodgers has done, and by the kind of spirit, not only in the Board, but in the student body.

"I think that the things the School is working with [in regard to its location in Ambridge] speak well about perseverance and dedication, and a real pursuit of things that are right for the Church."

God drew individuals from three countries and eight states to be part of the first TESM faculty and board of trustees, gathered here outside Hale Hall at Robert Morris College for the opening convocation on September 25, 1976.

Front Row, L to R: The Rev. Paul Zahl; the Rev. John Leggett; the Rev. John Guest; Dr. Leslie Fairfield; Dr. Peter Davids; the Rt. Rev. Alfred Stanway; the Rev. Peter Moore; Mr. Edward Abell, Jr.

Back Row, L to R: The Rev. Dr. John Rodgers; the Rev. C. FitzSimons Allison; Mr. Robert Crock; the Rev. Richard Lobs; Mrs. Dora Hillman; Mr. Samuel Abbott; the Rev. James Hampson, Jr.; Mrs. Joan Hay.

After months of fruitless searching for facilities of its own, and prayer that God would make it clear where He wanted the School to be located, TESM purchased this church in Ambridge in the spring of 1978.

In God's timing, a vacant supermarket across the street from the church offered room for a library and offices, as well as the needed parking spaces. The purchase prices of the church and the supermarket together almost exactly equaled the amount of money given over three years earlier to launch the School!

In another example of God's provision, two students in the first two classes had experience in construction, and were able to oversee the renovation of the supermarket, which was completed in the fall of 1979.

Bishop Alfred Stanway, first Dean and President of TESM, preached in Trinity Cathedral, Pittsburgh, PA on October 15, 1978, as his successor, the Rev. Dr. John Rodgers, was installed.

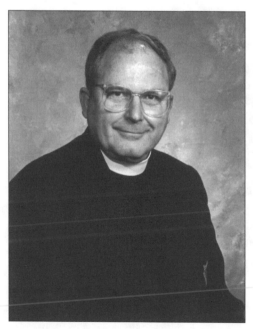

The Very Rev. Dr. John Rodgers, Dean/President of TESM from 1978 to 1990, ably guided the School through the process of accreditation to becoming a recognized and established seminary in the Episcopal Church.

Though they all came to Trinity without the sponsorship of any bishop or diocese, the first M.Div. graduates, shown here along with Board members, faculty, and field education supervisors on June 2, 1979, all found ministry positions before or shortly after graduation.

In March, 1985, the day after TESM had received tentative approval from the accreditation team of the Association of Theological Schools, an old warehouse only inches behind the library caught fire. As the Trinity community prayed to God to spare the School, the wind blew the flames in the other direction, and the library sustained only minimal damage.

In May, 1991, the Commons Building was completed,
providing needed classroom and meeting space. Trinity continues
to trust God to provide nearly 85% of the operating budget
through the donations of its supporters.

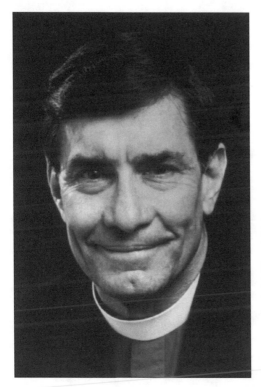

The Rt. Rev. William
Frey came from the
Diocese of Colorado in
1990 to take over as the
School's third Dean/
President. Under his
tenure, Trinity is
experiencing increased
growth and
effectiveness in training
lay and clergy leaders
for ministry.

11
Following God Every Step of the Way

B ig decisions had been made: the purchase of property; the selection of a new dean; the building up of the library; the accreditation process. But the whole time these larger issues were unfolding, there were smaller developments. It was no less important for Trinity to follow God's leading in each of these areas.

There was a continuing need for qualified teaching faculty. In each instance, Trinity has sought seriously to depend on the leading of the Holy Spirit in calling new faculty and senior staff. The Dean/President, faculty, and Board of Trustees review candidates, and they pray, expecting that God will lead them to a consensus.

Some of the new appointees have been interviewed at the suggestion of friends and colleagues in the Church. Others have come from different denominations. Most are ordained Episcopal priests, though a significant minority is made up of laypersons. And while they come from a variety of geographic, ethnic, and religious backgrounds, they all hold to a common understanding of the Christian faith as it is expressed in the School's Statement of Faith.

From the time it opened, Trinity offered its courses free of charge to students' spouses, either for credit or by audit. But most spouses worked outside the home full-time, or cared for small children during the day when courses were taught. Only a few were able to take advantage of the opportunity.

The School soon began to see the benefit of having couples enter the ministry as partners, even if only one of the pair were ordained. With the flexibility of being established in its own buildings, and able to set its own schedule, TESM began to hold a few classes in the evening, making it easier for spouses to study. It arranged the one-year lay studies program over a period of three years, so that interested spouses could leave Ambridge with a foundation in Christian studies.

One wife, who completed that diploma while her husband earned his M.Div., commented, "It has meant a lot to me to be able to study and grow while my husband was preparing for the ministry. I was afraid of stagnating while he was learning all these exciting new things, and then of being catapulted into a church as 'the minister's wife' without any sense of what my gifts were or of how I could carry out a supportive Bible-based ministry.

"But since I studied the basics of Christianity and of the life of discipleship, I've been able to lead Bible Studies and be involved in discipling relationships with individual women. I've known which areas of church life are challenging to me, and which ones hold no interest whatsoever. And best of all, I've been a team member with my husband, knowledgeable enough to be a sounding board for him about the ministry, and able to help him when he needs me to do so in the areas in which he is not gifted. Our marriage has been strengthened so that we can face the pressures of ministry together, and can be an example to the congregation of a faithful loving relationship."

The School has continued to grow in its support of spouses and families. It offers occasional seminars on marriage and the ministry. There are prayer meetings and small group Bible studies; these help spouses grow in their own spiritual lives, and equip them to lead similar groups in a parish setting. And there are counseling resources available to those who desire them. In response to God's leading, Trinity has sought to be a community which nurtures both students and their families.

Once Trinity had settled in Ambridge, and was no longer tied to the academic calendar of Robert Morris College, it seemed good to hold a January intersession. During that month-long term, those students who were not taking GOE's could choose intensive courses in ethics, or apologetics, or the Church Fathers. These electives would provide a change from the routine, and an opportunity for students to individualize their course of study.

This idea proved to be a positive innovation. Soon the program was officially named "January Term", and the number and variety of course offerings gradually increased. After three years, there was a growing body of Trinity alumni/ae, and these desired some continuing education, as well as a way to maintain ties with the School. The School was looking for more ways to promote parish renewal. The two needs were fulfilled together as JanTerm was opened to clergy and lay people around the whole Church. Involvement has grown steadily, and a June term has been added, so that four hundred participants a year now take the opportunity to study at TESM.

These short-term students are moved, not just by the content of the courses, but also by the joy of the fellowship and the vibrancy of the worship. The fact that people would travel to gray, snowy Ambridge in January indicates that, for many, JanTerm has become a "mountaintop" experience. For them, it symbolizes "going up to Jerusalem" to learn from God and to celebrate close fellowship with Him and His people.

As the School expanded, it needed to explore the implications of the guiding conviction that "money follows ministry". In general, the Episcopal Church recognized that seminaries needed to be in close contact with their supporters. The recent "1% resolution" requested parishes to give 1% of their budgets to the accredited seminary of their choosing. Even before the School was accredited, many parishes were donating 1% or more. Accreditation would surely boost the number of giving churches.

Trinity's sensitivity to the needs of its supporters was especially acute, because it relied on parishes and individual donors for 85% of its operating budget each year. As the School grew, and as its base of support did also, it became essential that communication be improved and the School's ministry enhanced. And so, in October of 1983, TESM added a Department of Church Relations.

As a result, Trinity developed closer ties with its supporting parishes. The School advertised and organized parish renewal weekends led by teams of faculty and students. The department worked on improving communications and publications, providing thoughtful articles, and letting supporters know how God was moving in the life of the School. It became a clearinghouse for job offers for graduates—every year there were many more requests for graduates than there were students available. It opened or reopened channels of communication with alumni through a newsletter. It labored in the area of development, making the School's needs known, expanding the number of donors to the School, and preparing proposals to foundations and potential contributors of large gifts for special or capital needs of the School.

As Trinity multiplied its ministry to churches across the country, support increased, and the School could continue to expand its efforts to train leaders for the renewal movement.

One of the Board's early goals concerned the development of a program of extension education. It became clear that Trinity's effectiveness as a "school for ministry" would be enhanced as it spread its resources to the wider Church.

As the Board and faculty traveled throughout the Episcopal Church, they became aware of a growing hunger in the person in the pew for an understanding of the Christian faith. At the same time, the national Church was producing few educational materials. Parishes were looking for resources from other denominations, or were struggling to design their own programs. Individuals were attending large conferences and buying cassette tapes as they sought Biblically-based instruction to help them grow in Christ.

In response to this perceived need, the School developed a new department, Trinity Episcopal Extension Ministries (TEEM). Remembering the Church Missionary Society principle, "Start small and follow God's leading", the initial committee sought to define a program, raise the necessary money from foundations, and call the right person to start up the ministry. Several individuals were considered but the doors remained closed until the summer of 1985.

John Rodgers was in Australia paying a sabbatical visit to the Stanways, when he just happened to meet the Rev. Ray Smith.

Ray expressed interest in the position, and visited the School that fall. As the committee members prayed and discussed the matter, it became clear that God was leading them to call him. Ray and his wife Shirley accepted that call, and moved to the United States the following spring.

TEEM's immediate priority was to design materials for parish adult education. During the late 80's, these were developed and marketed, with good response. TEEM also assumed leadership of JanTerm, and it was under its direction that the short-term residential education program grew so rapidly.

Later, four "TEEM 100" courses were drawn up as "Christian Foundations", a comprehensive introduction to theological study. They provided foundations in Old and New Testament Studies, Church History, and Systematic Theology. They were available to any interested person, but were particularly suited as a preparation for prospective students, giving them a head start on their degree program before they even moved to Ambridge.

TEEM's materials filled a definite need in the wider Church, and are still used, though not intensively marketed.

Since 1976, there has been a steady, but only gradual, increase in TESM's acceptance in the Episcopal Church. At first, a number of bishops would not allow evangelical students to come to TESM, ostensibly because it was not accredited. But since accreditation was first granted, more than half of the dioceses still do not allow students to come to Trinity, for whatever reason.

In addition, students who decide to come to Trinity as "free agents" have trouble finding dioceses to support them. They sometimes end up being delayed in the ordination process.

At the same time as it became apparent that enrollment in the M.Div. program was not experiencing a sharp jump following accreditation, God seemed to be leading Trinity to grow in a new direction, not to abandon, but to complement the M.Div. program. The Board and faculty explored the possibility of offering other degrees.

Within a few years, they had developed a Master of Arts in Religion (M.A.R.) program designed to provide training in academic theology for students who were not preparing for full-time pastoral ministry. It proved useful to those who were planning on doctoral work in theology or on teaching at a secondary level. A few people participated who were training for ordination in other denominations. Also, a steady stream of overseas students has chosen this course of study for its academic emphasis, finding it more relevant than the M.Div. program which focuses on training for pastoral ministry in North America.

With the success of this program, the School is preparing to offer master's level degrees in other areas such as youth work, evangelism, and missiology, following God's leading in regard to recruiting additional faculty with the appropriate credentials and gathering the necessary library resources.

One graduate commented, "The M.A.R. program has enabled me to understand the inter-related dynamics of Scripture, Theology and Church History in every area of ministry: personal devotions, lesson preparation for Sunday School, teaching series for adults, one-on-one discipleship training, personal evangelism opportunities, foreign missions awareness. In short, the M.A.R. program taught me the research methods and the 'research attitude' which will enable me to dig deep."

Though clearly committed to the authority of Scripture, Trinity is by no means a homogeneous body where everyone thinks the same way. Each year, the issues of churchmanship and women's ordination have brought new discussions, some more strident than others.

Though many of the School's founders were steeped in the Anglican evangelical tradition, faculty, students, and newer Board members have come from increasingly varied backgrounds. Some have been Anglo-Catholic, enjoying a more ceremonial style of worship, rich in ritual and symbolism. Others have experienced the charismatic renewal taking root around the country.

Since Scripture does not prescribe specific forms or ceremonies of worship, the Board has refrained from making a unilateral decision on churchmanship. Instead, Trinity's strong position on the centrality of the Gospel and the authority of Scripture has proven to be the unifying force. So the School has emerged, not so much as an evangelical seminary in the "low church" sense of the word, but as a rallying point of the evangelical/charismatic renewal in the Episcopal Church.

Peter Moore commented on the heritage of the School: "Alf Stanway brought the best tradition of Anglican evangelicalism to America. But our own evangelical heritage in the Episcopal Church had been dormant for so many years, we hardly knew what it would look like when it was Americanized. Our debt to leading Anglican evangelicals like Alf Stanway, and John Stott, and J.I. Packer, and Michael Green, and Festo Kivengere, and a host of others, was immense. But over the last decade, a genuinely American article has been reborn: radically Biblical in theological emphasis, gently charismatic in worship, strongly mission-and evangelism-oriented, integrating clergy and laity in joint ministry, and fueled by a desire to expound Scripture and proclaim the gospel."

Similarly, on the issue of the ordination of women to the priesthood, the School has gradually learned to cope with disagreement. Bishop Stanway taught that the Scriptures do not speak clearly on that subject and that, where godly people differ, it is important not to lay down the law. Since the stated role of the School is to train, not ordain, Trinity should be open to diversity, presenting students with the best arguments on both sides of the issue.

And yet, individuals in the TESM community—Board, faculty, and students—have continued to have strong feelings. The disagreement is not tidily divided between women and men; there are many men at Trinity who favor women's ordination, as well as some women who oppose it.

It has been the response of the School to welcome women into all aspects of the program and to seek to provide pastorally for the concerns of women wrestling with a call to ordained ministry. Some years, the composition of the faculty and the student body has caused the issue to consume much time and emotional energy; more recently, all incoming students have been clearly advised during the admissions process that, because the Church Canons allow women's ordination, they will be in classes with women who are preparing for ordained ministry. And the female M.Div. students are made aware that there will be some on the faculty and in the student body who are not in agreement with women's ordination.

Still, Trinity's **position** was perceived by many as a form of passive hostility because there were no ordained women on the faculty or the Board. In 1987, John Rodgers challenged the Board to interview and nominate qualified female candidates. The Board would never be able to come down unanimously on one side or the other of the issue. It was time for the School to recognize that it would have to continue to live with the two views held in tension.

Two ordained women, one of whom was an alumna, were eventually called to serve on the Board. And in 1989, the Rev. Mary Hays was called to fill a teaching position in the pastoral theology department.

For the most part, the prevailing attitude has been one of allowing differences to exist between believing Christians who seek to be guided supremely by Scripture. Ideally, what holds the Trinity community together in its diversity is the overarching mission to strengthen the evangelical/charismatic renewal in the Episcopal Church, and to bring the unchurched to know Jesus Christ in a saving way.

Sometimes Christians act as though they only need God's help, or can expect to see His hand at work, in "big" situations. And yet, there are always smaller decisions to be made as part of the ongoing process of faithfully serving Jesus Christ as Savior and Lord. In each instance, He asks individuals and institutions, "Will you seek to glorify Me today? Will you trust Me to reveal My will to you in this situation? Will you follow where I lead today?"

Trinity's leaders have found that the Lord doesn't always reveal His will in such dramatic ways as He did during the School's beginnings. Often, they have simply done the next thing next, following God every step of the way. And yet, God's work in the natural decision-making process, through individual believers committed to praying to know what is best and to doing whatever He blesses, has been no less miraculous.

12

Two Steps Backward, Three Forward

This particular "quiet day" seemed no different from others that the Trinity community had held. People took a break from regular classes to gather for a few hours of prayer and reflection at Mount Gallitzin Academy in Baden, a few miles down the Ohio River.

It was March of 1985. Three months earlier, the School had completed its self-study and had turned in its report to the American Association of Theological Schools. Now, a committee of the association had just visited Trinity to make its final evaluation. After numerous interviews and prolonged observation, the team had given a tentative "thumbs up" and had departed, with final approval awaiting the decision of the Commission on Accreditation of the ATS when it met in June.

The very day after this "exit visit", the community set aside time to give thanks to God. Students and faculty were grateful for His provision, especially for the rapid progress made in the development of the library. And along with thanksgiving for the apparent clearing of the accreditation hurdle, they experienced a sense of waiting on God for His leading for the next steps.

The stillness was shattered in the early afternoon when news came that the old box factory behind the library was on fire. Nine months earlier, that building had been purchased by the Pittsburgh Leadership Foundation. The foundation planned to renovate the block-long one-and-a-half-story shed according to Trinity's needs, and then lease it to the School. It would hold a badly needed commons area and would also provide office space for the growing number of Trinity ministries, all at a reasonable cost.

Now these future plans were literally going up in smoke. Not only that, but the factory was so close to the main building that the flames licked the back wall of the School. The gusty March wind threatened to spread the fire over the entire roof of the converted A&P.

Most of the Trinity community decided to remain in Baden to pray. Remembering that only a few weeks earlier, several people had died in a fire in an apartment building just blocks away, they prayed that God would protect everyone from injury. They asked Him to save the School building, and to prevent any damage from occurring to the library, which had been brought up to ATS standards only with large expenditures of time and money. They clung for encouragement to verses such as Isaiah 43:1, 2:

"But now, this is what the Lord says -
he who created you, O Jacob,
he who formed you, O Israel:
'Fear not, for I have redeemed you;
I have summoned you by name; you are mine.
When you pass through the waters,
I will be with you;
and when you pass through the rivers,
they will not sweep over you.
When you walk through the fire,
you will not be burned;
the flames will not set you ablaze...'"

Meanwhile John Rodgers and a few other faculty and students returned to Ambridge. Their hearts sank as they drove upriver. From several miles away, they could see black clouds of smoke billowing up into the air.

When they arrived, they rolled up their sleeves and began to help. Along with firemen from the fourteen different companies called in to control the blaze, they made repeated forays into the building to rescue library lists, office equipment, and files. And as they worked, they prayed, asking the Lord to turn the wind away from the building.

Within a few hours, the firemen got the blaze under control. In answer to prayer, the wind had indeed turned and had blown the flames away from the library. Not even the offices or student row houses closest to the flames had caught fire. **The main damage was** due to smoke and water. The School began restorations with gratitude.

Three weeks later, the Trinity community was preparing for a service of Holy Communion to be celebrated by the Rt. Rev. Alpha Mohamed, Bishop of Mount Kilimanjaro in Tanzania, East Africa. There was to be a festive reception following the service. Students and faculty alike were joyfully anticipating the Easter break that was about to begin.

The blare of fire sirens cut short the last of the preparations. People looked up at each other, instantly recognizing that they all had the same fresh memory of the fire that had come so close to destroying the School. Then, a student raced in with news that confirmed everyone's fears: "The box factory is on fire again, near the library end this time."

Once more, staff and students worked valiantly to save valuable equipment and records. Handfuls of Trinity people huddled together, asking God to spare the School once again, and to keep the books from being damaged by the dampness.

And once again, Trinity was protected from serious damage. The original renovations were delayed somewhat; the carpeting had been thoroughly soaked twice and had to be replaced, and the roof would have to be rebuilt. The recreation room area in the back of the building needed the most work. Some books from the Seabury-Western collection, waiting in storage until they could be catalogued, were destroyed.

But miraculously, there was no damage from fire itself. Twice, a building six inches away had burned to the ground, and Trinity had not caught fire!

Within a few months, repairs were complete, insurance money was available to replace the books with new purchases, and the School was continuing its normal operations.

As the leaders reflected on the near disasters, they began to see ways in which God's hand had been at work beyond the obvious sparing of the buildings. One immediate evidence was the enhanced relationship with the town of Ambridge.

Ever since Trinity had located in the former Presbyterian church and the A&P, the School's faculty and students had made numerous efforts to reach out into the community, some more successful than others. They had gathered food and clothing to distribute when the decline of the steel industry ravaged the town's economy. They had shared about the love of Jesus in door-to-door evangelism. They had offered services in the chapel to minister to townspeople. Individuals had had a positive impact in their neighborhoods, in their children's schools, and among local merchants.

Now the residents of Ambridge had an opportunity to minister to the Trinity community. They emerged out of their homes and cars to stand with students and staff, to express concern, to offer support and encouragement, and to marvel along with everyone else that the School never actually caught fire. A bond was forged in the fires, a bond which opened the way for later ministry.

The fact that the office/library building did not burn seemed to confirm the location of the School in Ambridge. Some had wondered whether this were only a temporary site for Trinity, just an intermediate stage in the process of starting a fully expanded seminary. They were afraid that in a run-down mill town setting, Trinity would not be able to attract "the brightest and best". By remaining in a blue-collar town in serious decline, was the School sending an anti-establishment message that would hamper its attempts to reach out across a denomination made up largely of middle- to upper-class people?

Many young people were moving away from Ambridge in search of jobs, leaving a population made up more and more of retirees. There was no guarantee that the town would survive in the long range. Who would move in when the older people died off? What industry would replace the defunct steel mills?

Plenty of students in the Episcopal Church were going to other seminaries. Was it because of Trinity's location?

About a half hour's drive from the School, a large Tudor stone mansion was for sale. Set on nine acres, with its slate roof, lead casement windows, and oak-paneled library, it exuded a style that complemented the traditional "Anglican ethos". Perhaps God wanted Trinity to relocate here.

Through the fires, God seemed to be saying, "No." If the building had burned to the ground, that might have been a green light to go elsewhere. But there were just as many good reasons to stay in Ambridge as there were reasons to move. And God had clearly preserved the building because He had more work to do in and through that place.

The original plan to renovate the box factory had to be abandoned, of course. In the months following the fire, Board members turned their attention away from that now vacant lot and began to focus on the half-block of property between the office/library building and the chapel. Here were the seeds of a clearly defined campus. Perhaps the School would be able to purchase the few remaining lots in the block.

The Board members began to dream. What would Trinity need in order to support a student body of up to one hundred and fifty full-time students? Many opportunities emerged: an endowed scholarship fund allowing more students to attend; a fund for professional development for faculty and senior staff; more support for TEEM to reach the wider Church; an institute for missions and evangelism, with an emphasis on church planting; the renovation and expansion of existing buildings; a commons building; a new faculty office building; the means to acquire and develop the properties for these proposed facilities.

And so, after several years of research and prayer, the School embarked on a capital campaign.

As always, Trinity's leaders were careful to go about their appeals for money in a way that honored God. They were open to professional fund-raising counsel, but were adamant in their commitment to continue to rely on the Lord for His provision. They wanted to make known their needs and dreams, to tell the truth about what God had been doing in and through the School without puffing up the facts and figures. They conscientiously wanted to avoid the manipulative pressures so often associated with such campaigns.

Called "Growing for Mission in Christ", the campaign had two stages. The Board members began by making their own pledges, and by making their needs known both to past donors and to individuals and parishes in the Pittsburgh area. During this "advance gifts" phase, $2.8 million was pledged.

The second phase, the public campaign, was announced in the spring of 1989, with the School hoping to raise an additional $3.65 million over the following fourteen months.

John Rodgers articulated the campaign's focus: "Consciously dedicated to spreading the gospel of Christ revealed in Scripture, we have unique opportunities and indeed, I think, unique responsibilities. After much prayer and reflection by everyone in the Trinity community, we decided that we needed to take certain steps to meet those responsibilities, and that we needed to ask our friends for support.

"We don't want to grow just to grow. We want to keep our simple lifestyle and keep ourselves open to God and our friends and supporters. But we do believe that God is leading us to grow in certain ways to further the mission He has given us."

By May 1990, ground was broken for a new commons building. That fall, the Stanway Institute for World Mission and Evangelism admitted its first students for a year's training.

A year later, the commons building was dedicated amid numerous expressions of amazement at how the School had grown and flourished in fifteen short years.

The fires had threatened to destroy the newly established School. Not only had the Lord protected Trinity from serious damage, but He had turned potential disaster into a source of blessing. What had seemed like a setback actually became a catalyst for further growth. Two steps backward had become in reality three steps forward under the sovereign rule of God. "Whoever is wise, let him heed these things and consider the great love of the Lord" (Psalm 107:43).

13
The Cross Held High in Ambridge

When the risen Jesus was about to leave His disciples for the last time, just before His ascension into heaven, He gave them a blueprint for the mission that they would undertake in His name: (Acts 1:8)— "You will receive power when the Holy Spirit comes on you; and you will be my witnesses in Jerusalem, and in all Judea and Samaria, and to the ends of the earth."

Jerusalem, obviously, was their immediate focus in bearing witness to Jesus. They would move gradually across geographic and cultural lines to the surrounding areas of Judea and Samaria. And eventually they would take the message with them wherever they went in the world. The spread of the gospel would take place in an ever-widening ripple effect. And subsequent history shows that that is exactly what happened.

Similarly, Trinity is having a growing impact, in the immediate town of Ambridge, in the Diocese of Pittsburgh, in national church organizations and affairs, and wherever its graduates are serving Christ in the world.

Soon after the school moved into its new buildings in the fall of 1978, word came of Cuban refugees being held by the thousands at Fort Indiantown Gap in central Pennsylvania. A student wife, Anne Ashley, heard of their plight, and began collecting donated clothes and toys in a storage room at the back of the partially renovated supermarket to take to the refugees. The response was good, and she was able to help many people, but it was a temporary need.

In the meantime, goods continued to pour in, furniture, housewares, clothing, linens. Anne sent some of them off to mining areas of Appalachia. Other things she boxed to ship to Uganda.

It soon became apparent that there were needs right in Ambridge and Beaver County. Anne set up shelves and racks and turned the storage room into a small shop. Word spread quickly in the local communities that this resource was available. Many people with no other connection to the seminary walked in and browsed, and took what they needed.

Nicknamed "Martha's Corner", the ministry flourished during the early 1980's when the steel industry in the Pittsburgh area began to falter. As more and more workers found themselves without jobs, and their families struggling, people stopped in, looking not only for supplies, but also for a word of comfort and encouragement. The Ambridge community was beginning to realize that Trinity was one of them, there to serve.

When Trinity moved to Ambridge, John Rodgers joined the Ambridge ministerium, a group of **clergymen** from many denominations seeking to work together to enhance the Christian unity and witness in the town. Through John, the School became involved in local affairs and spoke to issues affecting the community.

As the economic troubles worsened in the 1980's, the churches formed a C.A.R.I.N.G. Center (Churches of Ambridge Reaching out In the Name of God), providing a food bank, a place for needy women in the government's Women, Infants, Children program to pick up their checks, and job counseling, drug and alcohol counseling, and other social services.

Each year, in spontaneous but regular ways, small groups of faculty and students involved themselves in on-street evangelism and in going door to door, offering Christian fellowship and spiritual assistance. As expected, they met with varying responses. One woman even left John Rodgers and a student waiting on the front porch while she called the Trinity office to verify that "these two big men" were really who they claimed to be!

Gradually suspicions dissipated. Local residents grew to trust the Trinity community and to be grateful for the positive effect the School had on the local economy.

One day, eight-year-old Laura Vitunic asked her father Joe to accompany her class on a field trip to see the circus at the Civic Arena in Pittsburgh. Joe winced a little. It was his first year as a student at Trinity, and he was feeling the pressure of mid-term exams and papers due shortly. But he also knew that it meant a lot to Laura. As he prayed about it, he sensed the Lord urging him to chaperone the trip, so he accepted.

When he went to his daughter's school on the appointed day, he was asked to supervise fifteen second-grade boys. Joe settled into his seat in the middle of the bus, with his charges paired together in rows behind him. It wasn't long before a boy named **Jeremy** began to act up, using offensive gestures and profanity to provoke the other children.

Joe called **Jeremy** up to sit beside him and have a talk. He was ready to discipline **Jeremy**, but he wanted to learn a little about the boy first, so he gently asked him questions. One that popped into his mind was, "What do you like to do with your father?"

"My dad is a PIG!" **Jeremy** shot back vehemently. "And if he ever comes back, my mother and my grandmother are going to call the police!" He continued with a flood of stories, venting the rage and terror he felt for his father.

Joe was stunned. He had never heard a child with such strong hatred for his father. And he also felt deep compassion for the boy. When he commented on **Jeremy**'s behavior, he was firm but gentle, "**Jeremy**, I can tell you know the difference between right and wrong, and you know that what you were doing before was wrong. I want you to go back to your seat now and behave."

Joe watched him go back to his seat, and was startled when several other boys raised their hands frantically, begging to be the next to come up and "have a talk"! Over the course of the entire trip to and from Pittsburgh, twelve of the fifteen boys came up, unasked, to sit next to Joe. And one of the things Joe asked each boy was, "What do you like to do with your father?"

He discovered that ten of the twelve boys had no father living at home. It seemed to Joe that each child's story of pain and neglect was more poignant than the last. The whole incident weighed heavily on him.

Since their move to Ambridge, Joe and his wife Cindy had been praying and looking for ways to make their own children's adjustment easier. Now they began to pray for the needs of children without fathers. They shared their concerns with the other seminarians in their home fellowship group. Eventually they told the story to the whole seminary community gathered for a prayer meeting, asking the group to pray about ministry to children in Ambridge.

By Halloween of 1983, the Vitunics and a few other seminarians had developed "Kids' Club", an after-school activity for elementary school children. They drew up a flyer announcing the program and distributed it along with candy to Trick-or-Treaters. Over sixty children showed up the first day! And for the next three years, thirty to sixty children would come one day a week for crafts, games, music, Bible stories, and fun.

Soon parents of the children in the Club began to ask the Vitunics and the other seminarians, "Where's your church?" It became clear that it wasn't just the children who needed ministry, but whole families.

So, the following year, this core group started adult Bible studies and fellowship groups for the parents, to run concurrently with Kids' Club. The Vitunics also started an evening group in their home. Again and again, the question came up, "Where's your church?"

All along, Les Fairfield had been actively encouraging this budding ministry in Ambridge. He often met with the group in Joe's and Cindy's home to pray about the possibilities.

One day in the fall of 1984, it seemed clear to everyone in the group that God was asking them to worship together on Sundays. Right then and there, Les called Bishop Hathaway, and received his permission for the formation of this official fellowship. The new Church of the Savior met on Sundays in the Vitunics' living room for the next six months.

In March of 1985, they were outgrowing the living room, and prayed for a larger space. Soon they were meeting in the American Legion Hall rent-free! Les was priest-in-charge, and two African students who were priests took turns celebrating the Lord's Supper. The congregation limped along during this time. It was made up mostly of seminarians, and didn't grow much. There seemed to be trouble linking with Kids' Club families. And there was a lot of effort involved each week in trying to set up for a service in this non-traditional setting, only to have to take down all the furniture afterwards.

A crucial turning point came in 1986. Joe, and many of the core leaders of Kids' Club, were graduating from Trinity. Most others were moving on to ministries in other dioceses, but it seemed to Joe and Cindy that God was calling them to stay in Ambridge, and to continue in this work.

In a way, that "call" didn't make any sense because they had no idea whether or not the Diocese of Pittsburgh would provide any financial support. And yet, as they looked back, they could see several indicators during their seminary years, clues that hinted that God was behind this idea all along.

When they had moved to Ambridge four years earlier, there had been no rentals available, so they had bought a modest home. Now they remembered that they had each had a distinct impression way back in 1982 that they were investing in the community for a reason that would become known some time in the future.

Joe and Cindy had also learned dramatically during those years that God was able to provide for them and their three children. The money that they had saved to support their family while Joe studied ran out earlier than they had expected. But the Vitunics kept praying to God to provide, and being obedient to what they thought was His will. And the miracles began to happen!

Periodically, checks would appear in Joe's mailbox at school, donations from supporters of TESM who wanted to help students, but who didn't know anyone in particular. Every now and then, a consulting opportunity would arise for Joe, who was also a licensed professional engineer. They had no health insurance, but everyone stayed healthy. They were able to maintain their modest standard of living, even though they had no reliable source of income for eighteen months—none, that is, except for the Lord "who owns the cattle on a thousand hills".

Now, as they faced the challenge of remaining in Ambridge, they were not afraid to trust God to provide for them financially. They were willing to commit to ministry in the town; they just wanted to make sure it was His will. So they asked for clear guidance.

One of the things that concerned them was the need for some office space for counseling, administrative work, and group meetings. The Vitunic home had been the center of operations for a year and a half, but that situation was no longer practical.

Joe began to pray for an office and some meeting space. Within a few weeks, the Lord had led him to an apartment one block away from Trinity with six large sunny rooms. And the owner wanted the small church to have it rent-free! It was an exciting answer to prayer in and of itself, but it also confirmed to the Vitunics that God was indeed calling them to remain in Ambridge. That fall (1986), the church moved from the American Legion Hall into the Trinity chapel, where it has held Sunday services ever since.

Other ministries have grown out of the Church of the Savior. The Lazarus Center was founded to encourage growth and healing of the whole person (body, mind, and spirit), in the Name of Jesus. It provides, either on site or by referrals, Bible study, healing services, Christian counseling, twelve-step support groups, and physical wellness programs, as well as a list of physicians and psychiatrists committed to whole-person treatment.

Mary's Corner, named for Mary of Bethany who sat at Jesus' feet to listen, is open several days a week as a coffee shop where lonely people can drop in for conversation. Located near Martha's Corner, it has become a source of encouragement and fellowship for people who might never come to a church.

Ambridge Teen Ministries has been using some of the church's office space for its headquarters. Started by a former Trinity student, it is an evangelistic and discipleship ministry serving teenagers in

Ambridge in the name of all the Christian churches in the community.

With the combination of a visible, agreeable place to worship, and the clear leadership of one individual, as opposed to that of a group of seminarians, the church began to grow markedly. Six years later, the average Sunday attendance was approaching a hundred people.

Only a minority of the congregation was made up of students from Trinity. Most parishioners were from the Ambridge area, and fairly represented a microcosm of that community. There were young and old, lots of singles, several black families, and people with a wide variety of educational backgrounds and income levels.

Initially an outreach by Trinity students to local children, the Church of the Savior now provides open doors for people in Ambridge to come to know Jesus Christ personally, and to be part of the fellowship of His church.

14
Ministering in the Church and Beyond

With Bishop Appleyard's help, Trinity had quickly made a positive impact on the Diocese of Pittsburgh. Seminarians were serving in parishes; faculty members were working on various diocesan committees, and helping in parishes as interim clergy; graduates, even from the first two classes, were leading local churches.

When Bishop Appleyard called for the election of a bishop coadjutor in 1980, John Rodgers was one of the candidates. But the convention chose Alden Hathaway, whose personal spiritual renewal had paralleled the growth of Trinity.

Alden had not really been aware of the renewal movement when he was in seminary. Peter Moore had attended the same school, but Alden was told that Peter's ideas represented a little school of German pietism, and had nothing to do with Anglicanism!

More than ten years into his ministry as a priest, Alden was leading a parish plagued by divisions. A fellow clergyman confronted him with the need to simply preach the gospel. As they exchanged sermon notes, interacting with each other's comments scribbled in the margins, Alden came to a new faith and to a personal relationship with the risen Jesus Christ.

He attended the renewal conference in New York City in October of 1975, when Trinity held its first Board meeting. There he was introduced to Bishop Stanway, whom he invited to lead a retreat at his parish in Springfield, Virginia. Over the next few years, Alden traveled to the Pittsburgh area for conferences at St. Stephen's Church, and at the newly founded School. He would occasionally stay at the Stanways' home, bringing along various books donated by Jack Goodwin, the librarian at VTS.

After he was consecrated, Alden was elected to serve on Trinity's Board. Under his leadership, the Diocese of Pittsburgh has been most supportive of the School, accepting numerous graduates to lead local parishes.

Planting Churches

One of the leading thrusts of Alden Hathaway's episcopate has been the establishment and execution of a plan to start new churches. Two priests from the diocese were out in California in 1983, studying church planting at the Fuller Institute, when they noticed an elderly man putting coins in a parking meter. One of them recognized him as Donald McGavran, the "grandfather of the church growth movement".

They went up to him, and shared their excitement about the plan germinating in their hearts and minds. They had been inspired by the teaching in their seminars that church planting was the most effective way to reach the unchurched with the message of salvation through Jesus Christ. They looked at their own situation. In Alden Hathaway, they had a bishop who was willing to pay the price of leadership in this area, and to set church planting as a priority. Because of the diocesan structure, they were in a position to set goals that church planters from other denominations could not.

They asked Donald McGavran if he thought it were possible for a diocese in the Episcopal Church to have such ambitious plans. His response greatly encouraged them, "Any true branch of Christ's vine can bear fruit that will last."

Alden Hathaway endorsed with enthusiasm the plan to establish fifteen new congregations between 1984 and 1994. He articulated the vision for new churches in every corner of the diocese, through every committee. He marshaled resources of money and talent. He became a faithful pastor and encourager of new church pastors, believing it was crucial to evangelize and incorporate the unchurched.

By 1992, there had been nine new church starts, and three more were under consideration. Of the nine, six were still in existence, though one was no longer part of the Episcopal Church. The three that "died" had each lost a vision of their purpose, to reach the unchurched.

The role of the diocese was to get mission-minded parishes thinking about their neighbors and about the possibility of beginning a new church in order to reach them. Studies had shown that new people are far more likely to visit a new congregation than an existing one. In more established parishes, people tend to be need-driven. They often place their own needs ahead of those of the outsider, but the new church's reason for being is to reach those who have no church home.

So, in many instances, the local church became the church planter. The diocese would come alongside the parish, and stimulate a movement within that congregation to raise up leaders who shared the missionary vision. They would call an ordained person, and would together become the nucleus of a new congregation. This model always paid for itself; money and leaders would be replaced, following the teaching of Jesus, "Give, and it will be given to you..." (Luke 6:38).

Two other congregations were formed in urban settings. Recognizing that urban America waits to be reached with the gospel, and that Episcopalians have a poor track record, the Diocese of Pittsburgh made a long-term commitment to these new churches. It was clear that they might never be self-sufficient, but that the support was warranted nonetheless. Now the Diocese is even planning to establish a minority-specific congregation.

Of the nine churches that were started, six have been served by Trinity graduates. With the theological training that these students received, they learned to think biblically, and to ground their ministry in that theology. And the vision to reach the unchurched was fostered through the School's emphasis on sharing the gospel.

In recent years, especially with the founding in 1989 of the Stanway Institute for World Mission and Evangelism, Trinity has become more intentional about training students to plant churches. A course in church planting is one of the requirements for the Diploma in **Mission** and Evangelism. JanTerm courses have offered the teaching to the wider Church. And TESM is working with Episcopal Renewal Ministries to raise the awareness of Episcopalians around the country to a call to plant new churches.

The Rise of Parachurch Ministries

As one looks back, one can see God's hand at work in a way which no one foresaw or orchestrated. As John Rodgers and, to some extent, other faculty members traveled to churches around the country, sharing the gospel and encouraging many in the Church, they came to be involved on the boards of a number of different renewal ministries.

Since 1983, many of these parachurch ministries have moved their headquarters to Ambridge because Trinity was located there. God has blessed the School with their presence and their links with the ongoing work of the Church; in turn, these ministries have found their efforts enhanced through their association with TESM.

It began in 1983 with the arrival of the Brotherhood of St. Andrew, a long-standing ministry to men and boys. The Brotherhood seeks to develop, in local parishes, chapters of men who are committed to prayer, study, and service, in the name of Jesus Christ.

David Wilson, Executive Director from 1986 to 1992, deliberately focused on acquainting Trinity students with the ministry so that, when they left the Ambridge area, they would take with them an awareness of the Brotherhood as a resource for their ministry. Since 1983, many new Brotherhood chapters have been started, with a significant number led by TESM alumni/ae.

With the theological guidance of Trinity faculty and graduates, the Brotherhood has designed an evangelism training ministry called "Articulating Our Faith". Created to help reluctant Episcopalians learn how to communicate the essence of the gospel, it has been effectively used in parishes across the country.

In 1985, the Community of Celebration, led by the Rev. Graham Pulkingham, was praying about returning to the United States after a decade in Scotland. Bishop Hathaway invited the Community to consider moving to the Diocese of Pittsburgh.

Exploratory visits indicated to the leaders that the small city of Aliquippa, across the river from Ambridge, would be ideal.

Proximity to Trinity would be mutually beneficial, enhancing the teaching ministry of the Community and helping it to reach the wider Church more effectively with its music ministry.

The Community settled into Aliquippa several months later, buying property in the midst of the urban decay left by a declining steel industry. Seeking to reach out in its own surroundings, the Community worked with local citizens to expand the food bank of the Brotherhood chapter at All Saints' Church in Aliquippa into a region-wide food cooperative named Foodshare, now feeding over 12,000 people a month.

With a base in the United States, the Community's music team, the Fisherfolk, could travel more easily to American parishes for concerts. Composers Mimi Farra, who later became Music Director and adjunct faculty member, and Betty Pulkingham taught JanTerm courses at the School, helping students to become more aware of the role of music in liturgy, and spreading their resources of music for the renewal movement.

In 1988, Trinity's Trustees strongly urged the American branch of the South American Missionary Society (SAMS/USA) to move to Ambridge. Since the resurgence of that ministry in the mid-1970's, SAMS had sent many of its candidates to Trinity for some study in basic theology as part of their training for the mission field. The second stage of their program involved language training at SAMS headquarters in rural North Carolina.

This arrangement had worked well for nearly a decade, but the Lord was gradually making it clear that it would be better for SAMS to be situated near Trinity. The Society would benefit from sound teaching, close Christian fellowship, low costs, and proximity to the Pittsburgh airport. And the presence of a missionary society would help the Trinity community to be aware of the global nature of Jesus' Great Commission to go into all the world with the message of salvation.

The Rev. Walter Hannum and his wife Louise of the Episcopal Church Missionary Community (ECMC) had had a long association with John Rodgers dating back to John's years at VTS. Bishop Stanway had traveled out to Los Angeles to share with

ECMC and the Hannums about his experiences with the Church Missionary Society. The Hannums had, in turn, taught a JanTerm course on missions at Trinity.

As the School's Board prayed about developing a school of missions, it was led to invite the Hannums and ECMC to relocate to Ambridge.

Other ministries to be drawn by Trinity during the late 1980's were the Church Army, A Christian Ministry Among Jewish People (CMJ/USA), Youth Quest, Heartbeat Evangelistic Ministries, and Emmaus Ministries (a counseling and teaching ministry).

At the same time, there are ministries which, though not located in Ambridge, have nonetheless a loose link with the School. Senior staff and alumni have served on the boards of The National Organization of Episcopalians for Life (NOEL), Episcopal Renewal Ministries (ERM), Episcopalians United, and the Episcopal Synod of America.

It is significant that, in the Decade of Evangelism, there should be a rise in this "parachurch" movement, and a corresponding increase in the number of students training at Trinity for non-parochial ministry.

Addressing Controversial Issues

In the last few years, tensions have increased in the Church as issues about which Episcopalians care deeply have emerged to the forefront. Trinity as an institution, and individuals with links to the School, have addressed some of these, seeking to be guided by the Scriptures, and by reason and tradition as these are informed by faithful interpretation of the Bible.

They have stressed the uniqueness of Jesus Christ as the only Mediator between God and human beings. One alumnus, preparing to minister overseas to Muslims, went to another Episcopal seminary to meet with the missions committee of fifteen students, and found that the idea of presenting the gospel to Muslims was offensive to all but two.

But Trinity clings to Jesus' declaration that He is the way, the truth, and the life, and that no one comes to the Father except through Him. It is the most loving thing one human being can do for another, even for a Jew or a Muslim who already believes in one God, to help him or her to know the saving grace that comes only through faith in Jesus Christ and His atoning death on the cross.

In the area of human sexuality, the School seeks to articulate a belief based again on clear Scriptural teaching, on God's revelation of His will in creating the sexes, and on the general moral awareness of the human conscience. It upholds the position that sexual intercourse is given by God as a gift to be shared only between two persons of the opposite sex who are married to each other.

In regard to ministry issues, the Board passed a statement affirming "the historic belief that it is not appropriate for the Church to ordain an advocating and/or practicing homosexual or any person who is engaged in heterosexual relations outside of marriage." At the same time, it acknowledges the power of Christ to heal, and does not exclude from "fellowship and possible ordination those who are repentant, forgiven, and healed from such advocacy and practice".

In 1989-90, Trinity professors pored over the proposed inclusive language liturgies and decided that the School would not use them in worship. The following year, in the quarterly magazine *Mission and Ministry*, they warned of the spiritual dangers of, among other things, altering the Name, and therefore the character, of God.

Leaders associated with TESM have sought, not always successfully, to write and speak prayerfully, with charity and without the use of code words, aiming to be winsome and loving, yet bold. Through them, the authority of Scripture is once again becoming a legitimate position in the discussion of issues facing the Church. Sexuality happens to be the hot topic for the time being, but the ultimate controversy is over whether or not God's revelation in Scripture is going to be changed.

As Trinity becomes an increasingly effective brake on unscriptural tendencies in the Church, its leaders still realize that arguments do not renew the Church; Jesus Christ does. And so their ongoing commitment is to educate, nurture, and train leaders who know Jesus Christ and who can help others to know Him.

15
Far More Future With God

A s the 1980's came to a close, John Rodgers was looking ahead to the time when he would step down as Dean/President. He wished to teach theology, to write, and to remain actively involved in the life of the School, but he sensed it was time to make way for fresh leadership.

The Trustees went about this search in the same way as they had for all the other leaders that they had called to serve at Trinity, remembering the principle, "Under God, everything depends upon the quality of the people chosen for the task." They spent months praying and reviewing candidates. They interviewed a few, and spent a couple of days in discussion among themselves. And it seemed right to them to call the Right Reverend William Frey, then Bishop of Colorado, to be Trinity's third Dean/President.

Bishop Frey

Bill Frey can't remember a period when he didn't know something about Jesus. He recalls giving his life to the Lord many times as a young man.

When he was in his early twenties, he undertook an exercise in self-examination, diligently writing down several pages of notes in preparation for making his confession. As he became aware of his need for forgiveness and made his confession, he became truly aware of absolution as it was pronounced. He heard, really heard, the Gospel promise of forgiveness, and experienced deep freedom and joy as a result.

He went on to Philadelphia Divinity School (before it merged with the Episcopal Theological School to become Episcopal Divinity School), graduating in 1955. After his ordination to the priesthood, he served churches in Colorado, New Mexico, and Costa Rica before becoming the missionary Bishop of Guatemala in 1967.

111

Bill learned many lessons during those first few years as Bishop. He saw in tangible ways the power of the Gospel as "good news". He had always believed that it was useless to evangelize someone until you had met his or her physical needs. And while he still sees some validity to that approach, he was surprised to find that, even when he didn't have any way of meeting people's physical needs, they often wanted to hear from him about Jesus Christ anyway.

He saw firsthand that the message of Christianity accumulates cultural additions. These aren't necessarily wrong; they just happen. But it is important to realize that they are there and to allow them to be challenged by Christians from other cultures. The truth of Christianity is at the core, and it is the same everywhere, regardless of the cultural baggage that gets added on. It is the truth of the Cross that must be proclaimed.

From his time in Guatemala, Bill also began to see more clearly how the value system in American society had gone awry. He quickly learned that the Church is entirely separate from its buildings. He was consecrated Bishop of Guatemala in a large empty lot under some pine trees. And though there was no building, the Church was there, present in the people of Jesus Christ!

After a few years, the Freys were abruptly expelled from the country because Bill had publicly called for reconciliation. As the family regrouped in the United States and waited for the Lord to reveal the next step in Bill's ministry, he, his wife, Barbara, and some of their five children experienced a new turning point, a powerful time of renewal. It included greater surrender to God and correspondingly greater freedom in serving him.

Shortly afterward, Bill was called to be Bishop of Colorado, where he served for eighteen years. There he emerged as one of the leaders of the growing movement of renewal taking place within the Episcopal Church. He was an early supporter of Trinity, and one of the founders of the Episcopal Renewal Ministries.

Through his leadership in Colorado and as a clear and courageous defender of the Scriptural understanding of moral and theological issues before the House of Bishops, Bill learned to pray with people with whom he differed. He saw the need for brothers and sisters in the Body of Christ who disagreed on something to come together before God, realizing that they were each sinners in need of His grace. Instead of praying for God to straighten "them" out, Bill began to pray for "us", and not just for "them".

In 1985, he was one of four candidates whose names were put before the General Convention as a possible successor to Presiding Bishop John Allin. Three years later, he was again in a visible leadership role as he represented the Church in the daily press conferences during the General Convention.

The Trinity community welcomed the news of Bishop Frey's call to be Dean/President. There was a deep sense of a new beginning at the School. Bishop Stanway had died a few months earlier, and though it had been eight years since he had visited the United States, his passing signified to many the end of an era. The public phase of the campaign "Growing for Mission in Christ" was well underway. The years of consolidation under John Rodgers were coming to an end; a time of expansion was at hand.

Bill was bringing to Trinity the right ingredients for this new period. His gift of administration would be helpful, for as the School had grown, it had become more and more unwieldy. While it had been advancing on so many other fronts, it had sometimes lagged behind in administrative development.

As a bishop known and respected throughout the Church, Bill would bring an ability to communicate, not just with the School's natural constituents, but also with those who still did not understand Trinity. He would commend the School to those who were still on the fence.

The Freys had also spent many years living in community, inviting others to share their home. They knew the blessings and pitfalls of closeness with other Christians, and would be committed to paying the price to keep that sense of community a high priority at Trinity.

Since Bishop Frey has assumed the position of Dean/President, Trinity has been experiencing marked growth. More and more students are enrolling as the School makes rapid strides toward its goal of serving 150 full-time students. Funds are coming in to carry out the aims of the campaign "Growing for Mission in Christ". Buildings are being built, degree programs expanded, and new faculty called.

Best of all, people who were taking a neutral stance on the School are being won over to a more positive view. One bishop, who had originally felt that the Church didn't need another seminary, commented after a visit to Trinity, "Anyone discouraged about the future of our Church only need spend a day there to absorb the enthusiasm."

What Does the Future Hold?

What lies ahead for Trinity and for the Church which it seeks to lead further into renewal? Simply the continuing need to follow God every step of the way, adapting to new challenges as they present themselves.

Already, the School is a monumental testimony to what God can do. He kindled a desire and vision in individuals who were scattered geographically. He drew all these people together and helped them to unite around a common vision. He motivated them to pray. He made them into leaders, stretching them to begin accomplishing His purpose.

Through a sharing of the vision, He provided the necessary funding. He raised up Bishop Stanway, who knew how to start new ventures, and would equip the Americans to carry on. He drew faculty from unexpected sources. He helped them all to dream big, and start small. He guided them step by step through all the decisions that needed to be made.

He raised up students who were sure enough of their call so that they would be willing to risk not getting ordained. He provided a long-term facility. He called John Rodgers, under whose leadership the School grew strong and became accredited; John's gracious manner has commended Trinity throughout the wider Church and has helped it, at the same time, to cope with not being acceptable, by nature, to others. And He has chosen Bill Frey to lead TESM in expansion and increased effectiveness.

There is no telling what God will yet do through His people. The School is still young, and though its very existence speaks volumes about the movement of God in the Episcopal Church today, its most significant contributions lie ahead. As more and more alumni exercise mature Christian leadership, a momentum builds.

In the meantime, there is the challenge for the School to maintain its cutting edge, its distinctiveness. It was founded specifically as a School *for Ministry*, and not as a graduate institute of theology; it has begun to build a tradition of training men and women for spiritual leadership in the Church. Now it needs to continue that tradition, ironically, according to Mike Henning, without becoming traditionalist!

In this regard, it is crucial that the Board, faculty, and senior staff continue to hold high the vision and sense of calling, allowing them to be so compelling that other issues move to the back burner, placed in more realistic perspective. As the School is unified around its mission, it will go on training leaders to help others become aware of the living God.

What about the School's response to the changing relationship between the "Christian movement" and the secular culture? Les Fairfield wonders if Christians are losing the struggle to define American culture, as some say. If so, then Trinity will need to shift paradigms and develop new programs that train leaders, not for parish leadership based on a nineteenth-century model, but for leadership in an underground, confessing house-church movement. In fact, TESM is in a unique position to make such a transition because of its emphasis on training lay leaders as well as clergy.

If American culture does become completely redefined, the School will also need to build greater ecumenical cooperation with evangelicals and charismatics across denominational barriers. Denominational loyalties will not mean much. In many ways, Trinity and its community of alumni/ae and supporters have much more in common with orthodox believers of other denominations than with Episcopalians with liberal theology.

While some have lamented what they call "the good old days", before the School became "an institution", Steve Noll doesn't believe "there's any way that we can, or should, avoid the tension between vision, on the one hand, and institution on the other. We must be careful that we are not so enamored of tent-making that we ignore the riches and the values of institutional life. Nor should we become so institutionalized that we become offended by the simple acts of faith...or the 'untidy' people that God raises up and brings into our midst."

John Rodgers asserts that the bottom line is leadership. "Well-grounded, effective leadership," he says, "is the key to long-lasting renewal."

John Guest concurs: "The question of leadership is crucial. It is up to the leaders in the Trinity community to model the kind of leadership that will influence the next generation, and then to challenge people to pray about a call to ministry. Whenever we see youngsters in grade school, or junior high, or high school, or college, or even adults who are exercising some kind of leadership, we can nudge them into thinking about how God might be wanting to work through them. We must continue to attract strong leaders and train them, and give them a vision for what the Church can be."

Bishop Frey is hopeful and encouraging, both about the future of the Church, and about the role that Trinity will play in helping more and more people come to a personal relationship with the living God. Following a meeting in March of 1992 at the Kanuga Conference Center, where bishops gathered to relate to each other personally and spiritually, and not politically, he wrote to Trinity supporters expressing his conviction that healing had begun.

As "hot issues" were shelved, and bishops spent time in Bible study, prayer, and discussion in small groups, a sense of spiritual community was being formed. The new openness to each other that came through times of reflection was refreshing. There was an increasing desire to alter the decision-making process in the Church so that Episcopalians could move away from the divisions besetting them under the pressure from competing interest groups. While it will take time, and more meetings of the same nature, there is a new beginning.

Thinking back about the early history of Trinity Episcopal School for Ministry, Bishop Frey commented, "What a wonderful, countercultural thing the founders of this place have done, to go against the flow. They saw that a witness to Jesus Christ was vitally needed in the Church and the world, and they set about building one.

"I'm hopeful about the future. I think Trinity is an idea that God Himself has put in the hearts of the people, and we can only go forward with great strength and vitality. It will take a lot of prayer, but we have far more future with God than past."

Let God's people be encouraged. His hand is clearly evident in the life of Trinity. May those who have not seen His power for themselves look at what He has done in this School and know that the God of the Bible is One who cares about and is able to help anyone who comes to Him in trust and with a willingness to follow Him.

And let those who have known His power press on. God has not abandoned the Church. The best is still to come!

"O God of unchangeable power and eternal light: Look favorably on your whole Church, that wonderful and sacred mystery; by the effectual working of your providence, carry out in tranquillity the plan of salvation; let the whole world see and know that things which were cast down are being raised up, and things which had grown old are being made new, and that all things are being brought to their perfection by him through whom all things were made, your Son Jesus Christ our Lord; who lives and reigns with you, in the unity of the Holy Spirit, one God, for ever and ever. *Amen." (Book of Common Prayer, p. 540)*

16
Ministering in the World

Graduating seniors are an enthusiastic group. They feel such relief at finally coming to the end of three, sometimes four, years of intense study. In a sense, their lives have been on hold, and they're eager to get back into the real world to apply all the knowledge they have accumulated.

Trinity graduates invariably feel they have received a strong foundation in Biblical Studies. They have learned to think things through theologically, and appreciate knowing how to challenge some of the ideas floating around the Church. They have seen firsthand the importance of prayer and are committed to following God's guidance. But when they leave the School, they soon realize how much they still have to learn about leading churches.

Many new priests find that people are wary of change. Others grow discouraged at how long it takes for their congregations to trust their leadership. Some are called to communities with unusual needs, and find that the programs they learned will not be useful after all. By trial and error, and with the passage of time, alumni are gathering a growing store of lessons learned, an awareness of what works and what has not worked in parish ministry.

Laying A Foundation in The World

The Rev. Geoffrey Chapman (MDiv '79), Rector of St. Paul's Episcopal Church in Shreveport, Louisiana, is clear that the preaching of the Bible is the starting point for bringing a parish into renewal. He calls it "the rudder by which the whole ship of the parish is turned around." Effective sermons expose God's people to His Word, His will, His revelation. They are Biblical, Christ-centered, and challenging, opening up the text and letting it speak so that people can understand it. Then Christians can apply the Word to their lives, and grow in faith, in obedience, and in a closer relationship with God.

In some churches this emphasis is revolutionary. Sermons under previous clergy may have been personal reflections or social commentary, with or without a link to the Scripture reading. The Bible has not consistently been held up as the final authority in matters of belief and doctrine.

Sometimes the change is welcomed, but in other situations there is resistance. Particularly in the South, Episcopalians have traditionally chosen to be distinct from fundamentalists, especially Southern Baptists. Too much talk about the Bible or about personal faith is culturally contemptible. One alumnus discovered he was bucking this perception when a woman came to him and complained, "Why can't you talk about anything besides Jesus all the time?"

In some cases, a priest has been called to a church which has already tasted "renewal". Perhaps through Faith Alive or Cursillo, people have had spiritual experiences which have helped them feel loved by God, but have left them wanting to grow closer to Him. They may say that Scripture is important to them but their words and deeds and decisions show that they have not learned to think Biblically, to let the Bible be the foundation of their lives.

When the Rev. Ann Heinemann (MDiv '83) was called to be the Assistant Rector at St. Thaddeus' Episcopal Church in Aiken, South Carolina, parishioners were excited about her background in the renewal movement. But when she started talking about the authority of Scripture, they lost interest. They enjoyed informal services at their midweek gatherings, but they wanted these to consist of singing and Holy Communion, without Scripture readings or homily.

Because of her training at Trinity, Ann insisted on presenting even a short Biblical message. After six years, people are becoming accustomed to her practice and are accepting it. As they continue to attend conferences and retreats, they come across more and more leaders who teach from the Scriptures. They are realizing that that's what Ann has been doing all along.

For the Rev. Scott Quinn (MDiv '82), preaching was the only tool available for leading The Church of the Nativity in Crafton, Pennsylvania to healing and renewal. When he arrived there on a part-time basis, he followed a Rector who had served for seventeen years. Sunday morning attendance had dwindled from 250 to 30. Most parishioners were retired. There were less than five families with children. And Scott and his wife were the youngest adults in church.

People were angry and suspicious after having had a bad relationship with the previous Rector. Their one security was the familiar service. They didn't trust this new young clergyman whom the Bishop had appointed. They would not tolerate him meddling with their Rite I service. But they did admit that preaching was his domain. They even allowed him to lead them in singing "Turn Your Eyes Upon Jesus", but only as a preparation song before the sermon.

"So for the first three years," said Scott, "I preached and I prayed - it was all I could do. Eventually people stopped reading their bulletins and began to listen. They began to feel the presence of God in the church. And young people started coming."

Today there are 120-135 people at the Sunday service. There is a vibrant Sunday School and youth group. And the church has paid off its debt and keeps current with its bills.

Trinity graduates are adamant that it takes more than just Sunday morning preaching to elevate the ministry of the Word in their congregations. They have started Bible studies, even if only a few people are interested. They are convinced that when Christians feed on the Word, they grow to maturity. Biblically literate believers understand Jesus' desire to draw all people to Himself, and they begin to ask how He might reach others through them.

This Biblically-based vision is essential for entire parishes and not just for individual Christians. At Geoff Chapman's church, the clergy and vestry have worked together to articulate a mission statement with three commitments: that people would grow in commitment to the Lord, to fellowship within the church, and to ministries both inside and outside the church.

This decisive leadership is crucial if the church is to move from one place to another spiritually. Without a vision or goals, the congregation's agenda will be determined by circumstances and by complaining people. The saying is true, "The squeaky wheel gets the grease." When fault-finders see that there is a degree of power given to those who complain, they receive positive reinforcement for their behavior, and are apt to continue in it, to the detriment of the spiritual health of the congregation. Leaders must listen, and pray, and honestly seek to discern the Lord's will in the face of criticism. But then they have to proceed with what they believe to be God's plan, and not allow the church to be derailed from it.

Worship

If the ministry of the Word is a primary concern of Trinity alumni, the sensitive nerve of most Episcopalians is the style of the worship service. People on both sides of the alleged traditional/contemporary divide have strong, often non-negotiable preferences. So graduates have learned to move slowly with change.

Geoff Chapman encountered a distrust of "renewal" when he arrived at St. Paul's three years ago. A Faith Alive weekend nearly twenty years earlier had given some people a new awareness of the love of God. They had dabbled in "renewal", and were pressing for more informal worship with simpler "praise" songs. But the traditional people in the congregation didn't want any tampering with the service. They perceived "renewal" as a sideshow for a few freaks; it was fine as long as it remained on the fringes of parish life. As these attitudes had intensified, a growing barrier of judgmentalism was being built by both sides.

121

It has been Geoff's goal to "mainline" renewal by raising the level of worship in all three morning services. He wants all people to leave on Sunday morning, knowing that they have been with the risen Lord Jesus Christ in Word and sacrament. He has worked with layreaders, chalice bearers, acolytes, choir members and the Altar Guild to help them not just to lead worship, but to be worshippers themselves. As they carry out their functions in a spirit of devotion to Jesus, they set a tone that is caught by the rest of the congregation.

Geoff wants people to respond to the Word of God in the service, so he often invites them to do so at the time of Holy Communion. He might offer a specific instruction based on the message ("Come with forgiveness for someone who has wronged you" or "Come with a renewed dedication to follow Jesus Christ"). This has the effect of an altar call in a form more familiar to traditional Episcopalians.

He strives to hold gospel priorities, but to be flexible around the edges. For instance, he insists that each service have a sermon, but he encourages people to worship in ways that are comfortable and meaningful to them. If people want to raise their hands, they may. Likewise, if someone expresses devotion through genuflecting or crossing himself, he is welcome to do so. No one style is imposed, and neither are people judged for their preference. In this way, the leadership promotes unity to counteract the unhealthy degree of diversity.

At Ann Heinemann's church, the problem has been slightly different. The clergy leaders there have added services to intentionally accommodate diversity. The attempts to blend both traditional and contemporary elements into the main service had not worked. It seemed better to allow for individual preferences in worship, within limits. The goal is to lead each group into a deeper walk with Jesus Christ, wherever they happen to be at the moment.

Good Shepherd Episcopal Church in Norfolk, Virginia tiptoed hesitantly toward renewal when it called the Rev. Ross Wright (MDiv '81) to be its Rector in 1987. The church was in decline, with few young families with children. People saw that in order to survive as a congregation, they needed to risk moving in a new direction but they were still cautious.

Ross and his staff have deliberately cultivated a climate of prayer in the parish. They meet daily for morning prayer themselves, and plan the Sunday worship services in the context of prayer. The preacher tells what the theme of the sermon will be. Then the music, the prayers, even the bulletin cover, are all selected to undergird the Biblical message.

Ross has also established a Worship Committee whose primary purpose is to shorten the distance between the pew and his office. These people keep him informed about what nurtures and feeds the congregation. They also help the church to know that the Rector is sensitive to their preferences.

Through this communication, Ross has learned to honor traditions that existed before he arrived. For instance, if it were left up to him, he would not put the American flag in the nave, or sing national hymns. But these traditions are meaningful to a church situated only two miles from the largest military base in the country. So Ross has let them stand.

Proceeding carefully, Good Shepherd has introduced a more informal family service once a month. Piano and guitars are used to lead simple songs. New families have come in. And there are now 160 children in the Sunday School.

The Rev. Teresa Hunt (MDiv '88) has been leading a troubled congregation near Pittsburgh for nearly five years. She inherited a tradition of two Sunday morning services and, though attendance has doubled since she arrived, she has been trying to combine the two services so that the 75 people who attend will feel like more of a family. She has developed "Serendipity Sunday" to help people get accustomed to the idea.

Once every six to eight weeks, Sunday morning breakfast is served in the parish hall, followed by a simple Eucharist. More contemporary music is sung. The gospel is presented through a dramatic portrayal, and then the congregation forms small groups to delve further into the gospel under directed leadership trained beforehand by Teresa. This approach has attracted people, and has helped to raise the level of worship in the congregation.

Equipping The Saints for Mininstry

Clergy who have come out of Trinity have proven again and again the CMS principle that what matters most in a ministry are the people and the quality of their relationship to God. So, in the ways that are most appropriate to their congregations, they have poured themselves into developing lay leaders.

Of course, the foundation for this training is laid through preaching and teaching. As people get into the Word, they learn that God has given each of them gifts and abilities to use in serving Him. They want to discover what their gifts are, and how they can exercise them.

Ross Wright focuses some of this equipping ministry on the vestry. Newly elected vestry members are assigned leadership tasks appropriate to their gifts. They are expected to do more than just sit on a governing board. They become responsible for specific spiritual ministries. As they try to carry out these responsibilities, they often find themselves to be inadequate for the job, and come to the clergy for training.

Ann Heinemann has also found that people are open to teaching when they are faced with a challenge that seems too great for them. Her parishioners are sometimes asked to give talks at Discovery weekends, and are eager but feel overwhelmed. As they come to her for help in their preparation, she finds many opportunities to teach or counsel them, to pray with them for healing, and sometimes even to evangelize them.

In Geoff Chapman's church, a young couple began attending services when they moved into the area. The newlyweds had no significant commitment, but they were spiritually hungry and were open to Christianity. So when people from the congregation drew them in, they responded. They quickly met Jesus Christ and gave their hearts to him. They became excited and involved. They took evangelism training. They began bringing others to church. And they became part of a small group fellowship.

But they really came into their own by attending a discipleship program offered at another church. The program focused on health and diet and exercise in the context of Bible study, prayer, and accountability. The couple grew healthier and brighter, and moved forward in their walk with Jesus Christ.

They approached Geoff and asked if they could bring the program to St. Paul's. With his blessing, they offered the first twelve-week session. Twelve parishioners participated, and were enthusiastic about the effect in their lives. When the couple offered it again, forty people signed up. These newlyweds have really discovered their ministry.

In other parishes, lay people find their niche through hands-on experience, especially in social outreach ministries. At St. Mark's Episcopal Church in Bridgeport, Michigan, the Rev. Ken Bieber (MDiv '85) trained a laywoman in Bible Study, in prayer, and in the healing ministry of the Order of St. Luke. It soon became clear that she had pastoral gifts whose effectiveness could be extended through ordination. Now a deacon, she does most of the pastoral care in the parish. And she takes other people along with her to pray with the sick in the hospitals and to visit prisoners in the local jail. As these lay people see God working through their efforts, they are also trained to carry out those ministries.

Because St. Mark's is a small church - there are sixty families, and it has only recently received full parish status - it must choose outreach ministries carefully and do a few things well. They are now founding a group home to provide a safe loving environment to developmentally disabled adults. As they develop this outreach, not just for the sake of needy people but specifically to serve Jesus, they are seeing that God will work through the commitment of even a few people. And as the number of active lay leaders increases, the tone is set for others to be active themselves.

Finally, Trinity graduates are humbly seeking to model a life devoted to Christ. They realize that they became strong disciples of Jesus as they saw that attitude lived out by their teachers. Those who knew Bishop Stanway were profoundly influenced by his leadership. Their own experiences in ministry have brought to mind many of the Bishop's sayings and have served to illustrate them. The wisdom that they observed in him they are deliberately passing on to others.

In John Rodgers, they found an example of one who was completely committed to the gospel, who still handled distressing diversity with grace and a sense of humor. They learned from him that they didn't need to slap back every time someone slapped at them or at God.

In all of the staff, they saw a commitment to the lordship of Jesus Christ. He was the policy-setter, He gave the vision, and He provided the resources and power to bring the vision to pass. Remembering the impact of this devotion on their own lives has challenged Trinity alumni to live a discipleship that can be caught by those whom God has brought close to them.

Reaching The Unchurched

Under the Rev. John Burwell (MDiv '84), the Church of the Holy Cross in Sullivan's Island, South Carolina has experienced remarkable growth. When he was called in 1987, there were less than 100 members; now there are over 600. Before John went there, he told the search committee that God was not calling him to be a chaplain to a few families. They called him anyway. When he gave his first sermon at the church, he preached on Jesus' Great Commission in Matthew 28: "Go and make disciples of all nations..." And ever since then, he has been deliberate, even in a traditional congregation, about praying and working towards the growth of the church, both in spiritual depth and in numbers.

He has done this primarily by establishing an atmosphere of openness and friendliness, and by making the worship lively. Even though the main service at 11:00 a.m. follows the Rite I format, John and the assistant alternate the opening sentences and collects, making the first part of the service like a dialogue. He has trained the layreaders to understand what they're reading, to smile, and to keep their voices from being monotonous. He encourages the ushers to remember what it feels like to attend an unfamiliar church, and to make visitors feel welcome. As announcements are finished, he asks if anyone has anything else for the benefit of the church family.

With evangelism in mind, he has made the entire 9:30 service a children's service. He is intentionally targeting the people who feel that they ought to go back to church now that they have young children. These people are interested and open, mainly for the children's sake, but they dread having to sit through a long, boring service with squirming kids.

So John leads a full service for them, but it takes only a half hour. It's liturgy from a child's perspective, which thoroughly engages the young people. And the parents are glad to find something that their kids enjoy. Newcomers to this service quickly find themselves staying over for adult Sunday School and the 11:00 service.

In the pews, there are cards on which newcomers can fill out their names and addresses, and check a box requesting more information. When these cards are collected from the offering plate, a small team from the church will stop by the newcomers' houses that same afternoon. They make a quick, friendly contact, not even going inside, but just thanking the people for visiting the church, and giving them a welcome packet which tells about the church and the ministry opportunities available. John finds that when people are visited in this thoughtful but non-threatening way, they come back again and again.

The church's next venture is to start a Saturday evening

service, called "SOS" ("Sunday on Saturday"). While most of the visitors so far have had some kind of church background, the aim of this new service will be to reach the totally unchurched, especially those under thirty. It will be very different from the Sunday morning services, with a praise band, and contemporary music, and a Rite II communion service.

Who says a Rite I church can't be "renewed" and dynamic?

Church Planting

The Episcopal Church of the Word is a new congregation in Manassas, Virginia, thirty miles west of Washington, D.C. When the Rev. Alison Barfoot (MDiv '86) was called in 1991, there were six committed families who worshipped in the cafeteria of a Roman Catholic parochial school and rented office space over a bath products store. Under her leadership, membership has grown to eighty families and the average Sunday attendance has risen to 165 in less than four years. In December of 1993, after raising $300,000, the church purchased an existing commercial building, and remodeled it to house worship and education space, and offices.

As a new church vicar, Alison has wrestled with how to minister to unchurched people in a weekly communion service. She gives a modified instructed eucharist every week, inviting all to come forward at the time of communion to receive a gift from God. She welcomes all baptized Christians to receive the bread and the wine. If people are not baptized, she encourages them to come for prayer, urging them not to miss out on the blessing that God desires to give to each person present. Not all people come forward, but many do. Once a native American came to the rail, received prayer, and was reduced to tears by the sense of God's blessing.

At the Prayers of the People, where the Prayer Book allows prayers for individual needs, Alison encourages people to form small prayer circles of three or four. Those who would prefer to continue praying silently alone may do so, but most people join the circles. This practice has increased the congregation's awareness of God's presence in the service.

Because the Church of the Word does not have its own building, all activities outside of Sunday morning must be held in parishioners' homes. But Alison has capitalized on this limitation, and has focused her attention on developing home groups. She particularly values her training in small groups at Trinity, and is convinced that they are the place where real transformation occurs, including the equipping for ministry.

In these home groups, folks gather for prayer, Bible study, and sharing. Many of them live far away from their families, and crave the friendships they form in these groups. As they grow as Christians, they come to identify their spiritual gifts. These are further discerned and confirmed in the context of the home group, and in prayer and conversation with Alison. As people develop ideas for ministries along the lines of their gifts, they come to Alison to share them, to get her blessing, and to be turned loose. In this way, the ministries of the church are developing around the gifts and callings of the people in the church.

For example, there is now an active drama ministry among the teenagers, a sort of live Christian MTV. A group of people take a contemporary song, and dramatize it, complete with set and costumes and even "lip synching", and present it to others. In a church where 48% of the congregation is under the age of 18, this ministry has become an effective evangelistic tool.

Another obstacle Alison has learned to work around is the frenetic pace of life in Northern Virginia. Most parishioners spend three hours a day getting to and from work. They have to go to bed early, so they're not exhausted the next day. They are typically young families in which both parents work, so there are few volunteers from which the church can draw during the day. They have many competing demands on their time, especially if they have children with activities. It is difficult for them to commit to a sequential series of meetings or classes in the evening. So Alison often holds training sessions (for home group leadership, for example) in a long six-hour seminar one weekend, rather than in a six-week class. And she has broken major ministries into manageable chunks, letting people take responsibility for only as much as they can handle.

Through Trinity, Alison received a truly mission-minded perspective on ministry. She has, in turn, helped the members of her congregation, to see themselves as indigenous missionaries in greater Manassas. To use an analogy from business, instead of the members seeing themselves as the customers, with the priest there to serve them, the members see that the real customers are the unchurched in the community, and that it is the business of all members to take the gospel to them.

When The Programs Don't Work

By contrast, the Rev. Mark Lawrence (MDiv '80) has found progress to be slow and painful in a depressed area. He has led St. Stephen's in McKeesport, Pennsylvania for eleven years, and has seen it grow from about 150 people on a Sunday morning to nearly double that now. But growth has not come about in the ways he expected.

McKeesport was once a steel mill city, but it was already in decline when Mark arrived. People were discouraged. The city was deteriorating. Those who could find jobs elsewhere were getting out.

The average worker who stayed did not have leadership qualities. The mill had discouraged any entrepreneurial spirit in its labor force, and this lack of initiative had spilled over to other areas of their lives.

So traditional training programs met with little success, because they assumed that trainees would have a middle class background and education. Mark taught some people to evangelize. But when he tried to hand the leadership over to others, the program crumbled without his involvement.

He tried to get people to meet together in small groups, but they did not feel a need for fellowship. Many of them had extended families which served as small groups to them. Even though these family structures were not always healthy, they still kept people from experiencing the loneliness that more transient Americans feel.

And yet, the church has grown.

Mark has found that, because of the depressed area, people respond well to preaching that brings them hope, and assures them that God is with them.

He has found a Saturday service to be helpful. He started it because the Sunday morning service was too crowded. Also, it was an alternative option for a significant number of people who had to work on Sunday mornings. Over the last six or seven years, it has become a "feeder" service - many newcomers first come to that service, and switch over to Sunday morning later, as they become incorporated into the body. Part of the reason there has been a good response may be the fact that St. Stephen's is in a heavily Roman Catholic area.

Ironically, another source of the church's growth has been funerals. With an aging population, Mark conducts 25 funerals a year, an extraordinary number for a parish that size. When he preaches the gospel, and extends the loving care of God through the burial service, he finds there are many pastoral contacts afterwards. The message of hope draws people forward, and they feel they can come to Mark about specific problems. He counsels them, and many of them start coming to church, bringing their families.

For several years, St. Stephen's was also involved in a tri-church ministry, in which it was the strongest of three parishes linked together under a staff of three clergy. During that time, the congregation grew in outreach and awareness of others. It gained new members from a wider area, and became a regional church.

Now the Lord is leading St. Stephen's in three new directions. With unanimous approval, the vestry is setting money aside to enhance the music ministry of the congregation, making it traditional enough to sound like church, and contemporary enough to sound like the twentieth century. They are hiring a part-time youth minister to reach a growing population of teenagers. And they are advertising their presence through media and billboards.

With many obstacles, Mark has found that he has been called to exercise a faithful plodding, "a long obedience in the same direction."

Breaking Down Barriers

The Rev. Jim Pinto (MDiv '80) has also served an inner city church since he graduated, but he has faced a different set of challenges.

Until eighteen years ago, the health of Christ Episcopal Church in Fairfield, Alabama (part of Birmingham) ran parallel to that of the community. When U.S. Steel thrived (it once employed 20,000 people), and before desegregation became an issue, the average Sunday attendance was a comfortable 175. But as the steel industry faltered and Birmingham became a focus of the push for civil rights, the make-up of the community began to change. The population had been 80% white, but as whites moved out to the suburbs, it became 80% black. Attendance at Christ Church plummeted to 35 each week. And most of those people commuted in from a considerable distance.

Racial divisions have run deep in Fairfield for many years. As recently as the late sixties, no black was allowed to walk in the neighborhood where Christ Church is located. And there were parts of town where no whites dared to go. Blacks were even separated among themselves, and middle class whites wouldn't have anything to do with "white trash".

In 1977, the Rector, the Rev. Gilford Green, came to the end of his rope - and found personal faith in Jesus Christ. He began to lead the congregation in surrendering to Him, confessing sin, and receiving the power of the Holy Spirit. And the church started to look at its neighborhood and ask the question, "What would Jesus do?" One of the first answers was that people saw, with some trepidation, the need to reconcile with their neighbors.

Jim Pinto first went to Christ Church as part of a ministry team from Trinity that Gil had invited to lead a weekend at the church. In that short time, it became clear that Jim was gifted at evangelism and cross-cultural ministry. The congregation called him to come as an assistant when he graduated, but he would have to raise not only his salary, but also the money for any ministries he wanted to start.

When Jim asked himself the question, "What would Jesus do with my unique combination of gifts and talents?", he answered it by accepting the call, and by moving with his wife and three small children into the house next door to the church. That was the first step in developing an incarnational ministry. For he believed that people were crying out to see the love of Jesus Christ lived out in their midst by Christians who backed up their words with deeds.

At first, Jim just befriended people in the neighborhood. He started a Bible study, and began to be involved in people's lives. He was always inviting people to come to church. One black woman remembered being forbidden to walk near Christ Church - she had been so angry that she used to stand and throw rocks at people. And now she was actually being invited to church! She came to a service, and went forward to receive communion, but when the chalice came to her, she wouldn't drink. She was waiting for the separate cup for blacks. But as Jim explained to her that there was no second cup - that black and white were one in Jesus Christ - she drank. She got up from the rail, went down the aisle and out the door, and stood in the street shouting over and over, "We drink from the same cup, we drink from the same cup!" She continued to come, and invited her friends. She stayed, even though she was ostracized by many in the black community for associating with whites.

Week by week, it has been in worship that the ministry of reconciliation receives its motivation and power. Jim describes worship as drawing near and kissing the face of Christ. He sets the tone at the beginning of each service by speaking a few words to the congregation about why they're all gathered there - that is, as the priesthood of all believers, to attend to the Lord Jesus Christ, and to worship Him. They are not there to have their own needs met, but to magnify and bless Him, and to listen when He speaks.

The service of Holy Communion has continued to be a special place for racial reconciliation. And footwashing has also become a powerful sacrament. It is almost incomprehensible, especially for the elderly. But when descendants of Civil War soldiers and descendants of slaves demonstrate that they have accepted each other, they bear witness that the love of Jesus overcomes man-made barriers.

There is no specific program or strategy for equipping the saints for ministry. People who are new to the church are not immediately plugged into ministry. Instead, they are invited to worship among the community, to know Jesus, and to begin asking the question, "What would Jesus do if He were in my situation, with my unique combination of gifts and abilities?"

Newcomers who express interest in joining the life of the church participate in a fifteen-week class where they learn about the heritage of the Episcopal Church, about Biblical teaching, about the mission and ministry of Christ Church, especially since 1977, and about the intentional commitment to manifest reconciliation with Christ through the reconciliation of races and classes.

If they live away from the city, Jim invites them to pray about selling their homes and relocating near the church. He says, "Jesus didn't commute from heaven to earth -He came and lived among us." So far, about twenty-five families have accepted the challenge.

When people are ready for involvement in a social ministry, Jim encourages them to see one already in progress. Let them go into the soup kitchen to help out, and remind them, "These are our friends, these are our guests - welcome them in Christ's name." Or take a new Christian to witness a protest at an abortion clinic - it's like giving them six months of Sunday School all in one afternoon.

The question "What would Jesus do?" has been the crucial tool in overcoming the split between the propositional truth of the gospel and the living out of the gospel. Jim has found that, especially in the "Bible Belt", people can share the gospel verbally, and do so correctly, but they don't let it guide the way they live. Materialism is part of the problem. It's costly to sell a home in the suburbs and relocate to the inner city. It's painful to give up a lovely parish hall for a soup kitchen. The call to sacrifice runs against the grain of the acquisitive, comfort-seeking American way of life.

But as people have humbly and honestly faced the implications of being Christians, they have initiated many ministries. There is a soup kitchen which serves thirty thousand meals a year. A day care center staffed by formerly unemployed people, now trained, serves fifty to sixty children. A doctor in the parish has set up a clinic to provide medical care to the neighborhood. Shepherd's Fold is a halfway house for men coming out of prison. The Grace House is a home for teenage girls with crisis pregnancies. And nearly forty people, including Jim himself, have joined the pro-life rescue movement, have been arrested at abortion clinics, and have spent time in jail, doing what they believe Jesus would do.

Strategies for Coping

As Trinity alumni have led churches in knowing Jesus, they have picked up many "nuts and bolts" along the way. But they have all found that, regardless of strategies they may be applying in their ministries, they also need to have strong spiritual lives themselves. Perhaps the ordained ministry was once a high-status, low-stress position, but it is certainly the opposite today, especially for those seeking to bring about change in their congregations. Here is their advice:

Focus always on Jesus Christ, the Head of the Church, drawing closer to Him in regular repentance and confession. The moral and spiritual climate of the parish will only rise to the moral and spiritual level lived by the leader.

Despite occasional evidence to the contrary, continue to believe that people are hungry for your message. Keep the mission in view.

Pray, pray, pray. Set aside periodic days of prayer and fasting. Expect things to happen. Remember what God has done before - He can do it again. TRUST Him.

Though you might sometimes feel as if you are taking on the whole world all by yourself, avoid a "we/they mentality". Cultivate relationships, even with those who disagree with you. Spend time with people - let them see that you care.

Pray that the members of your staff aren't all discouraged at the same time!

Be prepared for the fact that many lay people bring into their relationships with clergy some baggage from past unresolved relationships, especially with their parents. They may act out of anger that is disproportionate to the issue. Don't take it personally, even as you seek to lead them to healing.

People may also have trouble trusting you if every other minister they've known has left after three or four years. Don't fight it. Earn the right to be heard. Be kind. Show up when you say you will. Rebuild trust, even if it takes years.

And always ask the question, "If Jesus were in my situation, with my unique combination of gifts and abilities, what would He do? How would He lift high the cross in this place?" Then do it.

APPENDIX
TRINITY'S STATEMENT OF FAITH

ARTICLE I   **The Holy Trinity**

The mystery of the Holy Trinity, namely, that the one God exists eternally in the three persons: Father, Son, and Holy Spirit; and has so revealed himself to us in the Gospel.

ARTICLE II   **The Lord Jesus Christ**

The full deity and full humanity of our Lord Jesus Christ, God Incarnate, who by reason of his birth of the Virgin Mary, sinless life, atoning death, bodily resurrection, glorious ascension, and triumphant reign, is the only Mediator between God and man.

ARTICLE III   **The Holy Scriptures**

The trustworthiness of the canonical books of the Old and New Testaments as "God's Word written," which contain all things necessary for salvation, teach God's will for his world, and have supreme authority for faith, life, and the continuous renewal and reform of the Church.

ARTICLE IV   **Justification and Sanctification**

The justification of the repenting and believing sinner as God's gracious act of declaring him righteous on the ground of the reconciling death of Christ, who suffered in our place and rose again for us; and sanctification as the gracious continuing activity of the Holy Spirit in the justified believer, perfecting his repentance, nurturing the new life implanted within him, transforming him into Christ's image, and enabling him to do good works in the world.

ARTICLE V   **The Christian Church**

The Church as the Body of Christ, whose members belong to the new humanity, are called to live in the world in the power of the Spirit, worshipping God, confessing his truth, proclaiming Christ, supporting one another in love and giving themselves in sacrificial service to those in need.

ARTICLE VI   **Spiritual Gifts and Ministry**

The calling of all Christians to exercise their God-given gifts in ministry, and to work, witness, and suffer for Christ; together with the particular call of ordained ministers, who, by preaching, teaching, and pastoral care, are to equip God's people for his service, and to present them mature in Christ.

ARTICLE VII   **The Gospel Sacraments**

The sacraments of Baptism and Holy Communion as "visible words" which proclaim the Gospel, and are means of grace by which faith is quickened and strengthened. In particular, the significance of the Lord's Supper as a communion in the Body and Blood of Christ, who offers himself to us in the action of this sacrament, so that by faith we may feed on him in our hearts and offer ourselves to him in gratitude for our salvation through his cross; Also, the openness of the Lord's Table as the place where all baptized believers, being one in Christ, are free to celebrate their common salvation in the Lord, and to express their common devotion to his person and his service.

ARTICLE VIII The Return of Christ

The personal return in glory of our Lord Jesus Christ at the end of this age for the resurrection of the dead, some to life, some to condemnation, for the glorification of his Church, and for the renewal of the whole creation.

Index